Brighter Child®
An imprint of Carson-Dellosa Publishing LLC
Greensboro, North Carolina

Brighter Child®
An imprint of Carson-Dellosa Publishing, LLC
P.O. Box 35665
Greensboro, NC 27425-5665

carsondellosa.com

Printed in the USA. All rights reserved.   ISBN 978-1-48380-135-3

01-034147784

Table of Contents

Math in One Minute 5
Place Value Riddles 6
Hopping Backward 7
What's the Difference? 8
Make It Half 9
Adding in Outer Space! 10
Subtraction 11
Missing Signs 12
Eight and Its Pairs 13
Frogs in a Well 14
Finding the Sum of Three Numbers 15
Which Unit? 16
Inch by Inch 17
Cups, Pints, and Quarts 18
Counting Minutes 19
Number Cruncher 20
Tricky Triangles 21
Find the Circles 22
Find the Squares 23
Slick Squares
   and Rowdy Rectangles 24
Shape Maker 25
Solid Figures 26
Shapes 27
All About Cubes 28
Tally Table 29
Detecting Dolphins 30
Line Plots 31
Venn Diagrams 32

Math in Three Minutes 33
Ladybug Lost 34
What Number Is Missing? 35
Missing Numbers 36
Missing Numbers 37
Counting Fish 38
Equal To 39
How Many All Together 40
How Many Left? 41
How Many Left? 42
How Many Pieces? 43
Check Your Skills 44

Just a Hop Away 45
Measuring Fun 46
Making a Prediction 47
"Weighting" in Line 48
Plus a Little More 49
Paper Clip Differences 50
How Much Space? 51
Telling Time 52
The Time Is? 53
How Long? 54
Reading a Bar Graph 55
Copycat 56
Twice as Nice 57
Halves, Thirds, and Fourths 58

Math in Five Minutes 59
Counting by Twos 60
One, Two, Three 61
Counting by Fives 62
Counting with Cookies! 63
Addition Problem Solving 64
Subtraction Problem Solving 65
More Than 66
Less Than 67
Number Construction 68
Great Groups 69
Simon Says 70
Petal Patterns 71
A Real Fashion Statement 72
Secret Code 73
Secret Code 74
Sum Search 75
Difference Search 76
Follow the Clues 77
How Can It Be Measured 78
How High Will It Go? 79
Which Holds More? 80
Filling a Box 81
Big Units and Small Units 82
Making Triangles 83

Answer Key 84–96

Introduction

Welcome to *Math in a Minute*! If you and your first grader find it difficult to fit extra math practice into your busy schedule, this book can help make the most of your time.

Math in a Minute is organized into three sections: One Minute Math, Three Minute Math, and Five Minute Math. Each activity supports the Common Core State Standards. The estimated time is based on the complexity and amount of steps it takes to complete each activity. The recommended time is only a guide. Select pages to complete based on the amount of time your child has for daily math practice. Encourage your child to work at his or her own pace and not rush through the activities. Then, you can identify areas your child excels in and areas for improvement.

Extra prompts are also included at the end of certain activities. These encourage your child to go beyond the problem and reason with the "why" behind math concepts. These prompts are not factored into the estimated time to complete the activity.

Math in a Minute Grade 1 includes these essential math skills:

- Representing and solving problems involving addition and subtraction
- Working with addition and subtraction equations
- Extending the counting sequence
- Understanding place value
- Measuring lengths indirectly and by iterating length units
- Telling and writing time
- Representing and interpreting data
- Reasoning with shapes and their attributes

Place Value Riddles

Read the riddles. Then, write the numbers.

Example: 2 4 5
ones
tens
hundreds

1. I have a 2 in the tens place and a 7 in the ones place.

   What number am I? _____

2. I have a 4 in the ones, tens, and hundreds places.

   What number am I? _____

3. I have no hundreds or tens. I have an 8 in the ones place.

   What number am I? _____

4. I have a 3 in the hundreds place. I have a 0 in the tens place. I have a 1 in the ones place.

   What number am I? _____

Hopping Backward

Subtracting is like counting backward. The frog is hopping backward. To solve the subtraction problems, draw the frog's path. The first one has been done for you.

1.

1 2 **3** 4 5 6 7 8 9 10   5 – 2 = 3

2.

1 2 3 4 5 6 7 8 9 10   6 – 4 = _____

3.

1 2 3 4 5 6 7 8 9 10   9 – 5 = _____

4.

1 2 3 4 5 6 7 8 9 10   7 – 1 = _____

5.

1 2 3 4 5 6 7 8 9 10   10 – 3 = _____

What's the Difference?

Subtract to find the difference. Then, draw a line to connect each equation with its matching picture.

1. 4 – 1 = _____

2. 6 – 4 = _____

3. 5 – 4 = _____

4. 5 – 2 = _____

5. 7 – 5 = _____

6. 6 – 3 = _____

Make It Half

Half means 1 of 2 equal parts of a whole. Answer the questions below.

1. An's mother had 6 pencils. She gave half the pencils to An and half the pencils to his brother Gan.

a. Color An's pencils red. Color Gan's pencils green.

b. How many pencils does An have? ☐ Gan? ☐

c. What number is half of 6? ☐

2. Bruce and Lisa's grandmother gave them 8 quarters. She told them to divide the quarters in half.

a. Circle Bruce's quarters. Put a box around Lisa's quarters.

b. How many quarters does Bruce have? ☐ Lisa? ☐

c. What number is half of 8? ☐

Do More: How do you find half of a group of objects? Write your answer.

Adding in Outer Space!

Find the answers. The first one has been done for you.

1.

$$\underline{4} + \underline{2} = \underline{6}$$

2.

$$\underline{2} + \underline{} = \underline{}$$

3.

$$\underline{} + \underline{} = \underline{}$$

4.

$$\underline{} + \underline{} = \underline{}$$

5.

$$\underline{} + \underline{} = \underline{}$$

6. Draw pictures.
Then, solve your problem.

$$\underline{3} + \underline{} = \underline{}$$

Subtraction

Subtract the kites by crossing them out. Write how many are left. Then, color the kites that are left.

$$\begin{array}{r} 9 \\ -\ 3 \\ \hline 6 \end{array}$$

1.

$$\begin{array}{r} 7 \\ -\ 4 \\ \hline \end{array}$$

2.

$$\begin{array}{r} 5 \\ -\ 4 \\ \hline \end{array}$$

3.

$$\begin{array}{r} 8 \\ -\ 2 \\ \hline \end{array}$$

4.

$$\begin{array}{r} 6 \\ -\ 1 \\ \hline \end{array}$$

5.

$$\begin{array}{r} 4 \\ -\ 2 \\ \hline \end{array}$$

6.

$$\begin{array}{r} 8 \\ -\ 5 \\ \hline \end{array}$$

Missing Signs

To complete the equations, fill in the missing signs. One must be an addition problem, and one must be a subtraction problem. The first one has been done for you.

1. 10 $\boxed{-}$ 4 $\boxed{=}$ 6

10 $\boxed{=}$ 4 $\boxed{+}$ 6

2. 12 $\boxed{}$ 4 $\boxed{}$ 8

12 $\boxed{}$ 4 $\boxed{}$ 8

3. 11 $\boxed{}$ 3 $\boxed{}$ 8

11 $\boxed{}$ 3 $\boxed{}$ 8

4. 10 $\boxed{}$ 5 $\boxed{}$ 5

10 $\boxed{}$ 5 $\boxed{}$ 5

5. 9 $\boxed{}$ 4 $\boxed{}$ 5

9 $\boxed{}$ 4 $\boxed{}$ 5

6. 7 $\boxed{}$ 3 $\boxed{}$ 4

7 $\boxed{}$ 3 $\boxed{}$ 4

Do More: Say each problem on this page using words.
Example: ten minus four equals six; ten equals four plus six.

Eight and Its Pairs

Look at the pictures and write an equation. Then, look at the equations and draw a picture for each one. Solve the equations.

1. (baseballs) + (baseballs) $4 + 4 = 8$

2. (footballs) + (footballs)   _____

3. (soccer balls) + (soccer balls)   _____

4. $7 + 1 =$ _____

5. $2 + 6 =$ _____

6. $5 + 3 =$ _____

Do More: All together, there are 9 different number pairs with a sum of 8. Can you list them?

Frogs in a Well

Five frogs hopped out of an 8-foot well. Sometimes, they fell backward, but eventually, they all made it out. Look at the equations. Draw each frog's path from the well. The first one has been done for you.

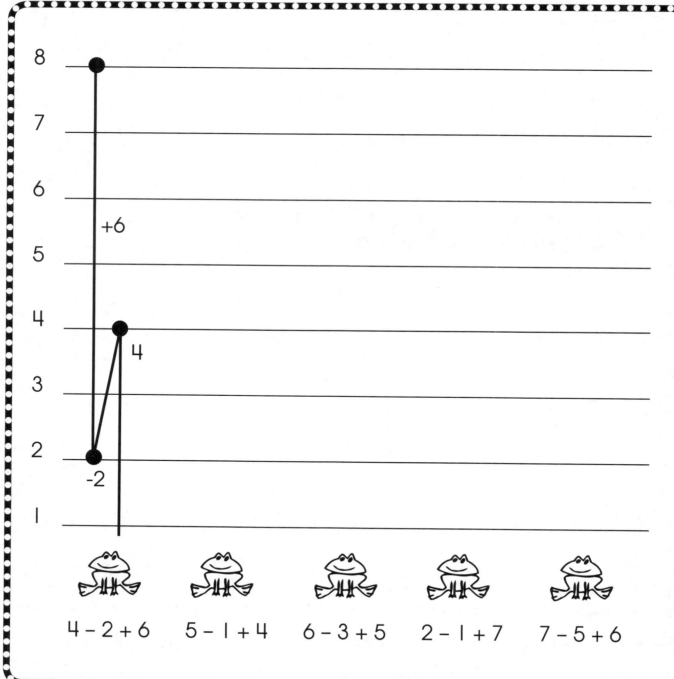

4 − 2 + 6   5 − 1 + 4   6 − 3 + 5   2 − 1 + 7   7 − 5 + 6

Circle the 2 numbers in each problem with a sum of 10. Then, add the last number. The first one has been done for you.

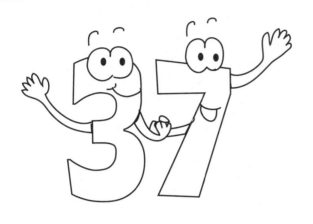

1. $\boxed{3 + 7} + 3 = $ _____

$10 + 3 = 13$

2. $1 + 9 + 3 = $ _____

3. $4 + 8 + 2 = $ _____

4. $7 + 3 + 6 = $ _____

5. $6 + 7 + 4 = $ _____

6. $2 + 8 + 9 = $ _____

Which Unit?

Which tool can you use to measure? Circle the best choice.

1. How much does this jar hold?

2. How tall is this doll?

3. How much water?

4. How heavy is this bag of candy?

5. How short is this castle?

Inch by Inch

How long is each object? Fill in the missing numbers on the rulers to find out.

1. The pen is _____ inches long.

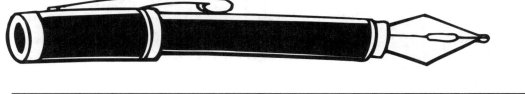

0   1   2   3   4   ☐   6

2. The shovel is _____ inches long.

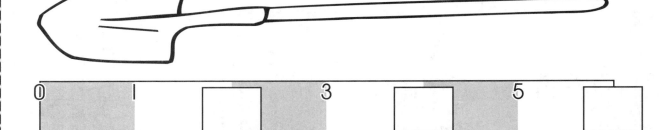

0   1   ☐   3   ☐   5   ☐

3. The chalk is _____ inches long.

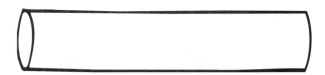

0   1   2   ☐   ☐   ☐   ☐

Cups, Pints, and Quarts

Circle which holds more.

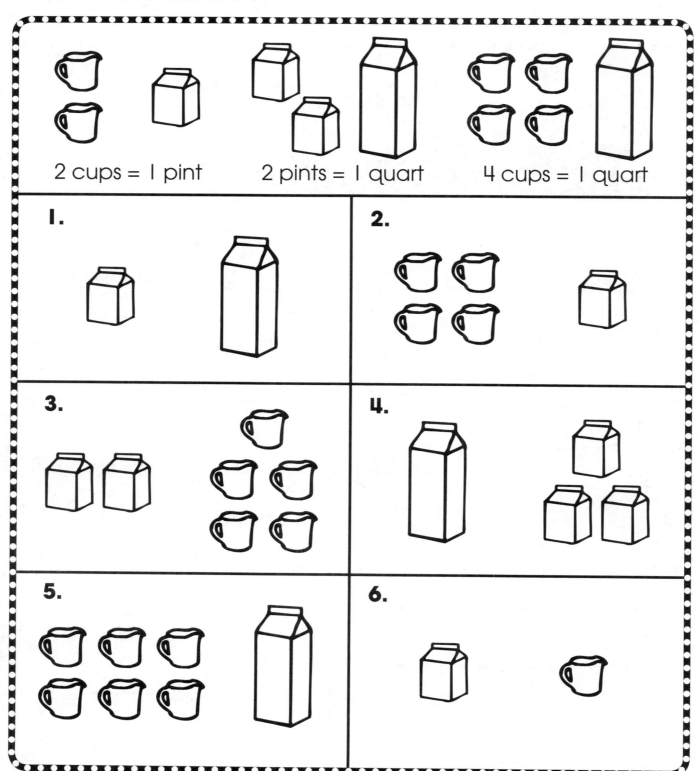

2 cups = 1 pint   2 pints = 1 quart   4 cups = 1 quart

1.

2.

3.

4.

5.

6.

18

Counting Minutes

Look at the clock. There are 60 marks around the edge. There are 60 minutes in an hour.

The long hand on a clock points to these marks. When it points straight up, it is at 0 (or o'clock). Count around each clock to the minute hand. Write the number of minutes on the line.

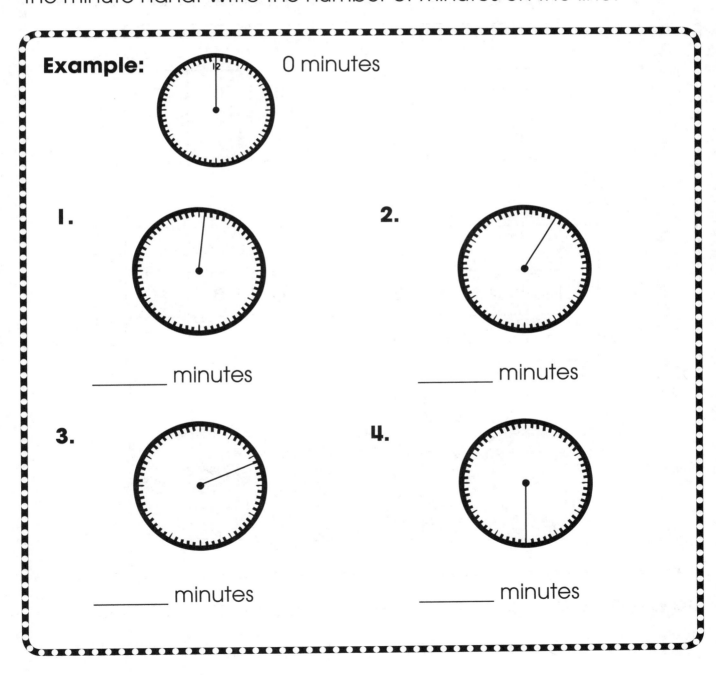

Example: 0 minutes

1. _____ minutes

2. _____ minutes

3. _____ minutes

4. _____ minutes

Number Cruncher

The number shrinker uses rules to change numbers. Put a number IN and a different number comes OUT.

Look at the rule in each chart. Use it to fill in the chart. Look for a pattern.

1.

Rule: + 2					
Number IN	1	2	3	4	5
Number OUT	3	4			

2.

Rule: + 3					
Number IN	2	4	6	8	10
Number OUT	5	7			

Do More: What number patterns can you find in each chart?

These shapes are triangles.

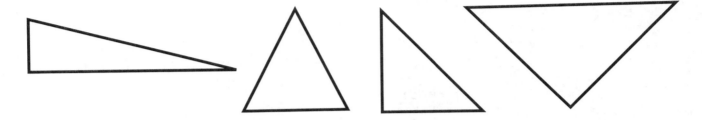

I. How many sides does a triangle have? _____

2. How many corners does a triangle have? _____

3. Look for triangles in the picture below. How many triangles can you find? Color each triangle.

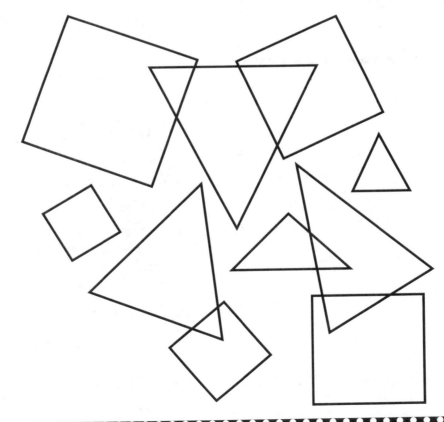

Find the Circles

Directions: Color all the circles you see in each picture.

Do More: Name an object that you can draw that is shaped like a circle.

Directions: Color all the squares you see in each picture.

Do More: Draw a picture that has a square in it.

Slick Squares and Rowdy Rectangles

These shapes are **squares**.

1. How many sides does a square have? _____

2. How many corners does a square have? _____

3. Which has more sides, a triangle or a square? _____

These shapes are **squares**.

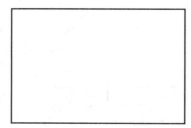 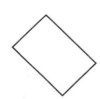 

4. How many sides does a rectangle have? _____

5. How many corners does a rectangle have? _____

Do More: How are squares and rectangles the same? How are they different?

24

Shape Mixer

Directions: Count the shapes in the blender. Answer the questions.

1. How many ☐ s?

   _____

2. How many ◯ s?

   _____

3. How many ▯ s?

   _____

4. How many △ s?

   _____

Write the name under each figure.

A **solid figure** is a 3-dimensional shape.

| cube | rectangular prism | cone | cylinder | sphere |

1.

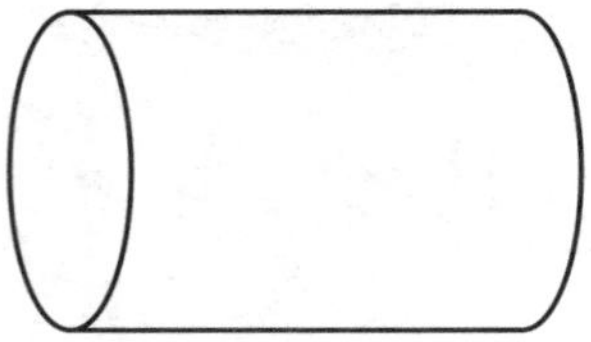

_____

2.

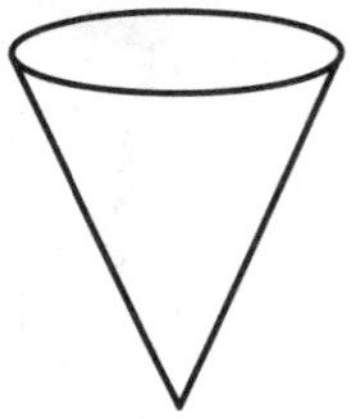

_____

3.

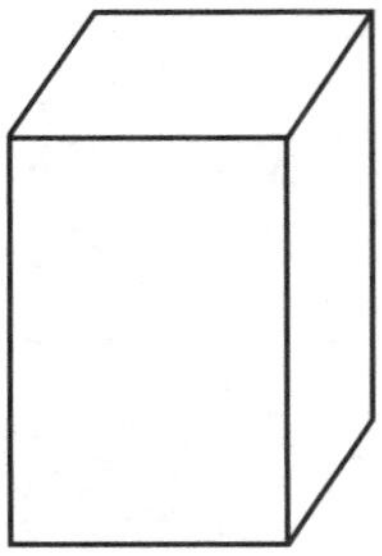

_____

4.

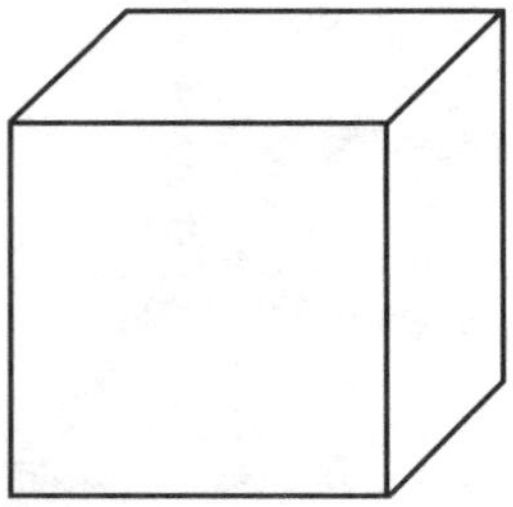

_____

5.

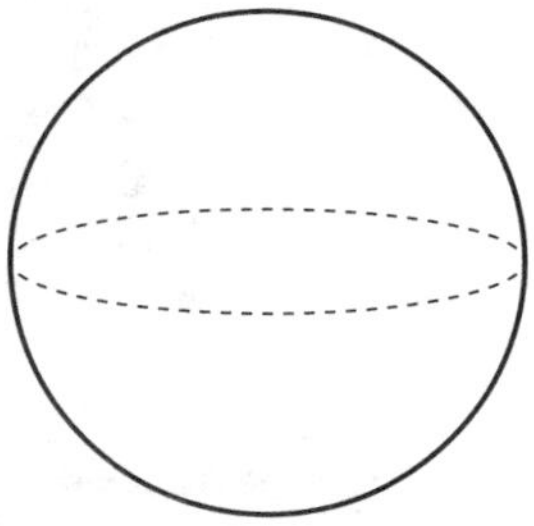

_____

6.

_____

Match the solid shapes on the left to the objects on the right. Write the names of the shapes on the lines.

1.

_____

2.

_____

3.

_____

4.

_____

All About Cubes

These solid shapes are **cubes**.

A solid shape has faces instead of sides. Find a cube, such as a block or a dice. Use it to find the answers.

I. How many faces does a cube have? _____

2. What shape are the faces? _____

3. How many corners does a cube have? _____

4. How is a cube different from a square? _____

_____

Do More: How are solid shapes and plane shapes (triangles, squares, circles, and rectangles) different?

Tally Table

Ms. Jamison asked her students, "What is your favorite recess activity?" She made a **tally table** by putting a mark next to each student's favorite activity.

(jump rope)	|||
(basketball)	卌
(swimming)	卌 |||
(hopscotch)	||||
(blocks)	卌 ||||

1. How many students are in Ms. Jamison's class?

_____

2. Which activity did most students choose? _____

3. Which activity did the least students choose?

_____

Detecting Dolphins

A pictograph uses pictures to show how many.

Jada and Jeff like to go sailing with their grandfather. In one weekend, they saw many dolphins.

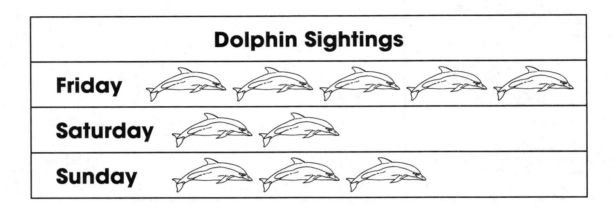

Dolphin Sightings

Friday	🐬 🐬 🐬 🐬 🐬
Saturday	🐬 🐬
Sunday	🐬 🐬 🐬

1. How many dolphins did they see on Saturday?

_____

2. They saw _____ more dolphins on Friday than on Saturday.

3. How many dolphins did they see all together? Write a number sentence.

_____

Do More: How is a pictograph like a tally table? How is it different?

Line Plots

A **line plot** shows numbers on a line. It is kind of like a bar graph.

Each X means 1 child. Use the line plot to answer each question. The first one is done for you.

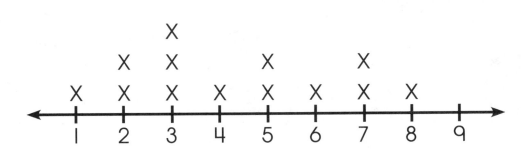

Mrs. Smith's Grandchildren's Ages

1. How many Xs in all? _____

2. How many Xs over 1? _____

3. How many Xs over 6? _____

4. How many Xs over 3? _____

5. What is the biggest number with an X? _____

Venn Diagrams

Look at this Venn diagram.

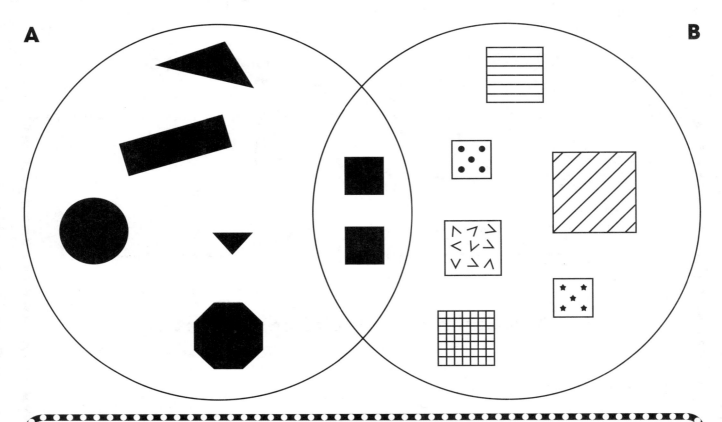

1. What is the same about all the shapes in circle A?

   _____

2. What is the same about all the shapes in circle B?

   _____

3. How many shapes fit into both circles? _____

Do More: Tell why the black squares can be in both circles.

Ladybug Lost

Help the ladybug find her way home. Fill in the missing numbers. Start at the number 1.

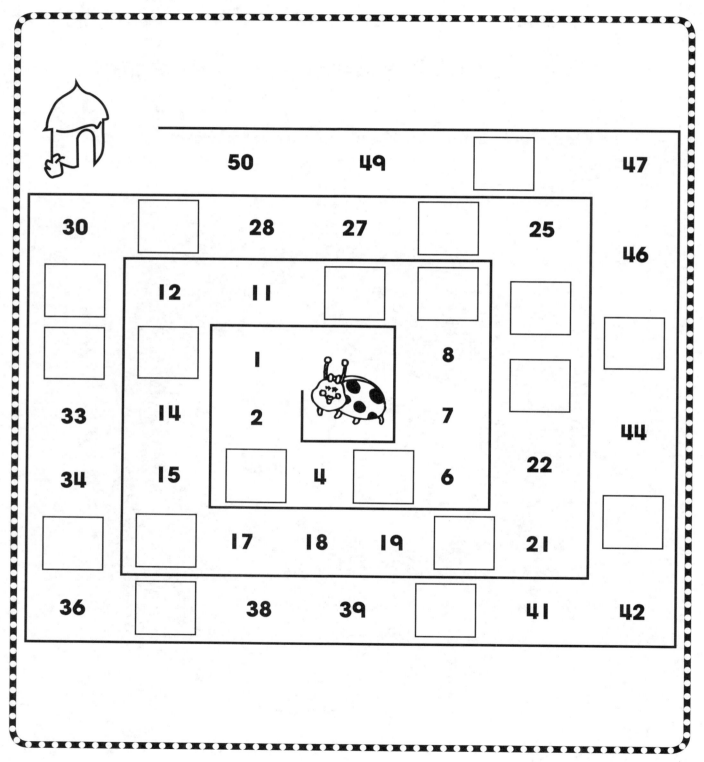

What Number Is Missing?

Write in the missing numbers.

6, 7, ___8___

1. 6, _____, 8   8, _____, 10   7, _____, 9

2. 5, _____, 7   _____, 2, 3   _____, 5, 6

3. 1, 2, _____   _____, 7, 8   _____, 3, 4

4. _____, 8, 9   _____, 6, 7   2, _____, 4

5. 4, 5, _____   2, 3, _____   7, 8, _____

6. 3, _____, 5   _____, 8, 9   4, _____, 6

7. 5, 6, _____   3, 4, _____   1, _____, 3

8. 8, 9, _____   _____, 4, 5   _____, 9, 10

1. Ms. Martin had a box of lost hats. On Tuesday, she found 3 more lost hats. She counted 7 hats all together. How many hats did she have on Monday ?

        Monday   Tuesday

  a. Draw the missing hats.

  b. Write the number sentence. ☐ + ☐ = ☐

2. Some brown bears are hungry. They join 5 black bears. Now there are 9 bears all together. How many brown bears are there?

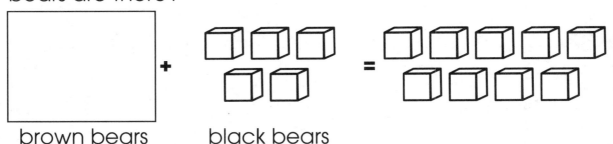

    brown bears   black bears

  a. Draw the missing blocks.

  b. Write the number sentence. ☐ + ☐ = ☐

Do More: What words tell you to use an addition problem?

1. The clown at the zoo held 7 balloons. Some of the balloons got loose and floated away. He counted 2 balloons left. How many balloons floated away?

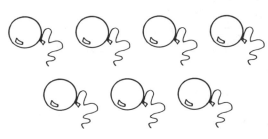

   a. Cross out balloons until only 2 are left. How many did you cross out? _____

   b. Write the number sentence. ☐ − ☐ = ☐

2. There is a stack of 10 pancakes. Oliver ate some. There were 4 pancakes left. How many did Oliver eat? _____

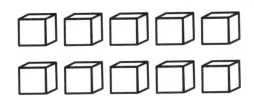

   a. Cross out counting blocks until only 4 are left. How many did you cross out?

   b. Write the number sentence. ☐ − ☐ = ☐

Do More: What words tell you to use a subtraction problem?

The arrow (<) always points to the smaller number.

5>3   **3<5**

5 is greater than 3.   3 is less than 5.

Complete the number line.

1	2			6				

3>2   **3<4**

Write > or < in the blanks. Use the number line to help you.

1. 5 ___ 2   1 ___ 7   1 ___ 9   8 ___ 5

2. 3 ___ 4   9 ___ 3   8 ___ 7   2 ___ 4

3. 6 ___ 5   5 ___ 3   5 ___ 7   3 ___ 5

Equal To

Find 2 ways to write each number. Write the number sentence.

1. The number 6

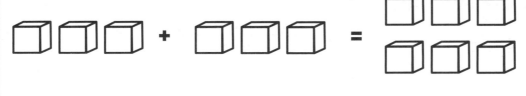

_____ + _____ = _____

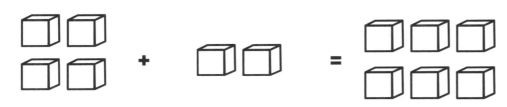

_____ + _____ = _____

2. The number 8.

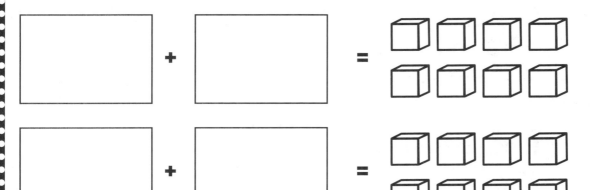

_____ + _____ = _____ + _____

1. Chito and Miguel went to a pet store. Chito chose 5 fish. Miguel chose 4 fish. How many fish did they buy **all together?**

a. Draw the fish. Count all the fish.

Chito

Miguel

b. Write the number sentence. 5 + ☐ = ☐

2. Angela ate 3 cookies. Cary ate 4 cookies. How many cookies did they eat **all together**?

1	2	3	4	5	6	7	8

a. Start on 3 and **count forward** 4 spaces. You will end

at number ☐ .

b. Write the number sentence. ☐ + ☐ = ☐

Do More: What kind of number sentence do you use to find how many **all together**?

Many Left?

1. Kessie's rabbit had 6 babies. She finds homes for 3 of the babies. How many babies are **left**?

    a. Cross out the 3 rabbits that have homes. Count the rabbits that are left.

    There are ⬜ rabbits left.

    b. Write the number sentence. 6 − 3 = ⬜

2. Dave has 8 trucks. He gives 3 old trucks to his little brother. How many trucks does he have **left**?

1	2	3	4	5	6	7	8

    a. Start at 8 on the number line. **Count back** 3 spaces.

    Dave has ⬜ trucks left.

    b. Write the number sentence. ⬜ − ⬜ = ⬜

Do More: What kind of number sentence do you use to find how many **left**?

Materials: 100 chart and counting blocks

1. Al has 19 baseball cards. He sold 14 to his friend. How many cards does Al have **left**?

   a. Use the 100 chart. Color the number 19 red.

   Count back or count forward?

   Count ☐ spaces. Color the number you land on blue.

   Al has ☐ baseball cards left.

   b. Write a number sentence. ☐ – ☐ = ☐

2. Theo has a box of 14 chocolates. Christa eats 5 chocolates. How many chocolates does Theo have **left**?

   a. Use counting blocks. Count out 14 blocks.

   Add 5 blocks or take away 5 blocks?

   Count the blocks now. Theo has ☐ chocolates left.

   b. Write a number sentence. ☐ – ☐ = ☐

Do More: Tell a story for this number sentence.

Solve the problem. $9 - 4 = $ ☐

How Many Pieces?

Stella has 18 pieces of candy. She wants to share the candy with friends.

---

1. Stella wants to give 3 pieces of candy to each friend. Circle groups of 3 pieces. Count the number of groups.

   a. How many friends get candy? _____

   b. Will there be any candy left over? _____

2. Stella wants to give candy to more people. Should she give fewer pieces to each person, or more pieces to

   each person? _____

3. What if Stella gives each person 4 pieces? Make each group of 4 pieces a different color.

   a. How many people will get candy? _____

   b. Will there be any candy left over? _____

Do More: Should Stella give 3 or 4 pieces to each friend? Why?

1. Draw blocks to make the scale balance.

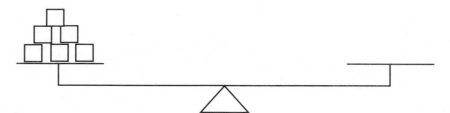

2. Write + or – to make each number sentence true.

a. 5 ◯ 6 = 11   **c.** 7 ◯ 2 = 5

b. 9 ◯ 2 = 7   **d.** 4 ◯ 6 = 10

3. Write >, <, or =

a. 8 ◯ 5   **c.** 10 ◯ 12

b. 6 ◯ 6   **d.** 7 ◯ 3

4. Circle all the numbers that could be the mystery number.

a. I am > 8. I am < 13. What numbers could I be?

1	2	3	4	5	6	7	8	9	10	11	12	13	14	15

b. I am > 2. I am < 7. What numbers could I be?

1	2	3	4	5	6	7	8	9	10	11	12	13	14	15

a Hop Away

Frannie Frog must cross 12 lily pads to get to the other side of the pond.

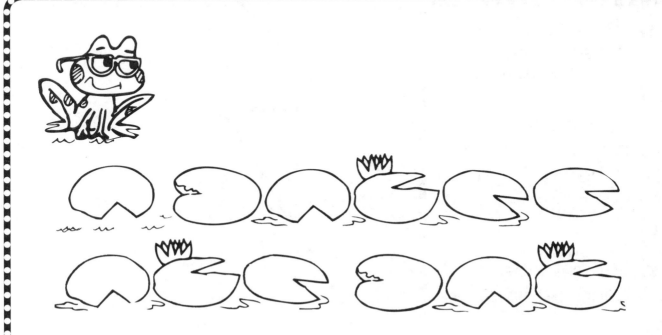

1. Frannie Frog jumps on every third lily pad. Color each lily pad Frannie Frog jumps on green.

2. How many jumps will she make to get to the other side?

   _____

3. Frannie turns around to head home. She jumps on every second lily pad. Color each lily pad she jumps on yellow.

4. How many jumps will she make to get back?

   _____

Measuring Fun

Find the answers below.
Foxy is running a race.

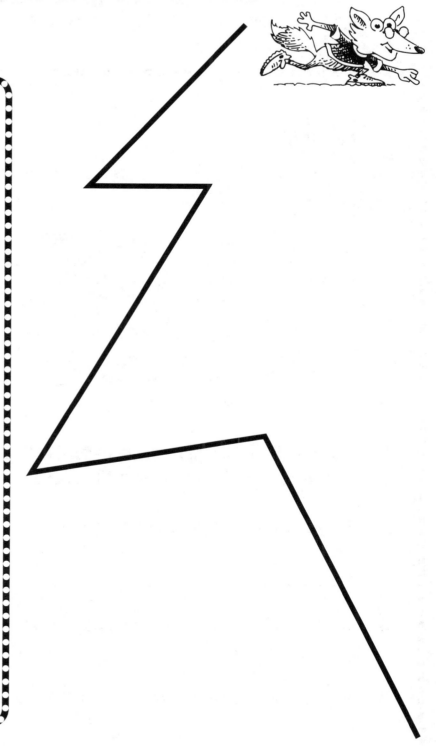

I. Use small paper clips to measure how far he runs.

How many paper clips long is the trail?

_____

2. Measure the trail using centimeters.

How many centimeters long is the trail?

_____

3. Which way of measuring was easier? Tell why.

How many centimeters long is a paper clip? How could you use this information to find the trail length in centimeters, without measuring? Write your answers on a separate sheet of paper.

1. Find two containers. Draw the two containers.

2. Use a piece of yarn. Measure how big around on two containers. Predict: Does the one that is bigger around hold more?

_____

_____

3. Tell how you checked it out.

_____

_____

4. Does bigger around always mean it holds more?

_____

_____

Do More: Put three containers in order from biggest around to smallest around. Then put them in order from holds most to holds least. Talk about what you noticed.

1. Look at the three objects below. Which do you think is heaviest? Which is lightest? Which is in the middle? Number them 1–3 to show lightest to heaviest.

_____   _____   _____

2. Choose three items in your house. Guess what order they go in.
Guess:

lightest   heaviest

Prove it. Weigh the objects.
Actual:

lightest   heaviest

Plus a Little More

How long is the snake? See that its head does not match up with the tiles.

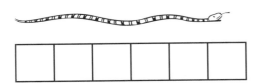

1. The snake is longer than 5 tiles. It is shorter than 6 tiles.

   What can we call that length? _____

   Let's make a rule: Count the number of units that are **mostly** covered.

Use this rule to name the measurement of each critter.

2.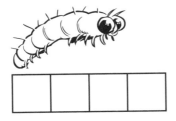

_____ units

4.

_____ units

3.

_____ units

Paper Clip Differences

Directions: Next to each length, write the number of small paper clips that fit on the line. Then write a math sentence in the box that shows the difference between the two lengths.

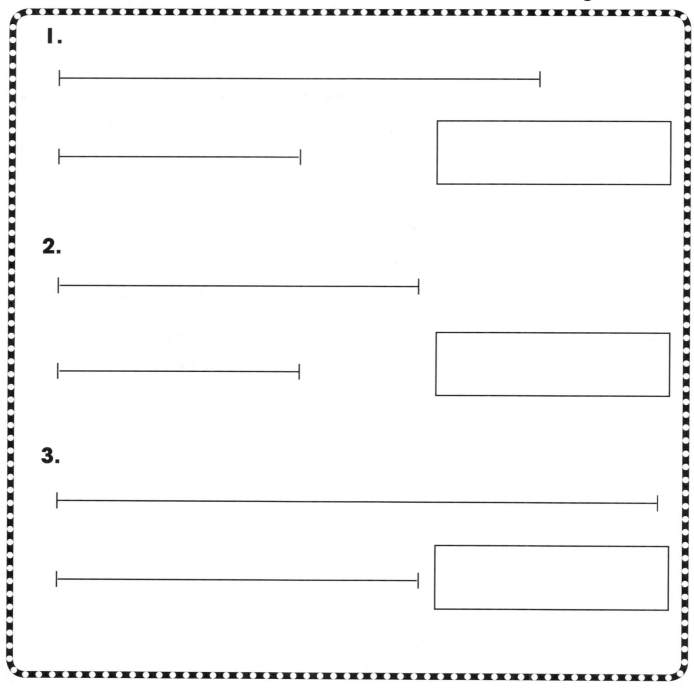

Do More: Would it be easy to measure things using only paper clips? Why or why not?

How Much Space?

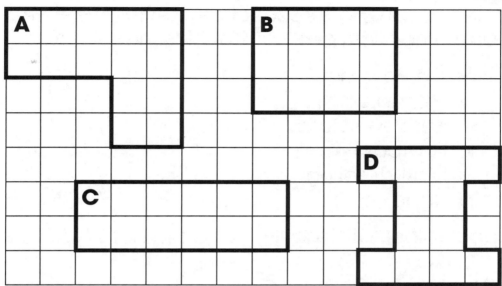

1. Look at the shapes. Estimate.

    a. Which shape has the most space? _____

    b. Which shape has the least space? _____

    c. Do any of the shapes have the same amount of space?

2. Count the squares in each shape to check your estimates.

    Shape A: _____   Shape B: _____

    Shape C: _____   Shape D: _____

3. How close were your estimates?

Do More: Use grid paper. Draw 2 different shapes that have the same space. Tell how you did this.

Peter is always busy after school and on the weekends with sports and other activities. Look at his schedule below.

7:30 A.M. Homework
10:00 A.M. Piano Lessons
12:30 P.M. Karate Lessons
4:00 P.M. Football Practice
6:30 P.M. Math Tutoring
9:15 P.M. Reading

Label each clock with the time and the activity it is showing.

1.

_____

_____

2.

_____

_____

3.

_____

_____

4.

_____

_____

5.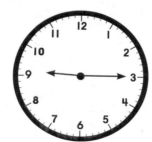

_____

_____

6.

_____

_____

The Time Is?

1. Kenny's birthday party started at 1:00.

   a. Show this time on the clock.

   b. The party ended at 4:00. Show the time on the clock.

   c. How many hours did the party last?

2. Eric's soccer game starts at 10:00.

   a. Show the time on the clock.

   b. After the game, Eric watched his brother's game. He left at 1:00. Show the time.

   c. How many hours was Eric at the soccer field?

Start Time

End Time

Start Time

End Time

Do More: How did you find the number of hours?

1. The parade started at 9:00 A.M.

Start Time

a. Show this time on the clock.

b. It lasted 2 hours. Show the time the parade ended.

c. How did you solve this problem?

End Time

2. Misha went to the park to play. She played for 3 hours with her friends. It was 4:00 when she went home.

End Time

a. Show this time on the clock.

b. What time did Misha get to the park?

c. How did you solve the problem?

Look at the **bar graph**. Use it to answer the questions.

Most Popular Subjects

	Math	Reading	Science	Writing	Social Studies

1. How many students enjoy Writing the most?

_____ students

2. How many students like Reading and Science the most?

_____ students

3. Which subject is the most popular? _____

4. How many more students like Reading than Math?

_____ students

5. Which subject is the least popular? _____

6. How many students like Science, Writing,

and Social Studies? _____students

Copycat

Directions: The part of the pattern that repeats is shown. Draw the pattern.

1.

☐ ☐ ○ △

2.

5 7 0 7

3.

9 9 3 5

4.

S P H T

5.

△ ○ ☐ ○

Which pairs of patterns are the same?

_____

Do More: How could you check your pattern to see if it is drawn correctly? Use one of the patterns to show how.

Double means add the same amount again.

1. There are 5 triangles. How many triangles will there be if the amount is doubled?

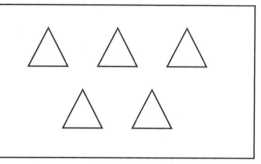

Draw 5 more triangles in the empty box.
Count all the triangles.

Finish the number sentence: 5 + 5 = ☐ .

2. What number is 4 doubled?

1	2	3	4	5	6	7	8	9	10

a. Use the number line. Start on 4.

Count ahead ☐ spaces.

b. Write a number sentence. ☐ + ☐ = ☐

Do More: How could you use counting blocks to find double an amount?

Halves, Thirds, and Fourths

How many equal parts are in each shape?

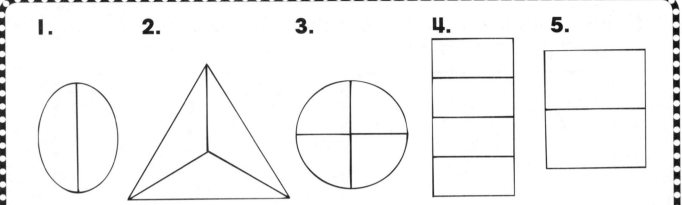

1. 2. 3. 4. 5.

_____ _____ _____ _____ _____

If a shape has 2 equal parts (halves), color it red.
If a shape has 3 equal parts (thirds), color it blue.
If a shape has 4 equal parts (fourths), color it green.

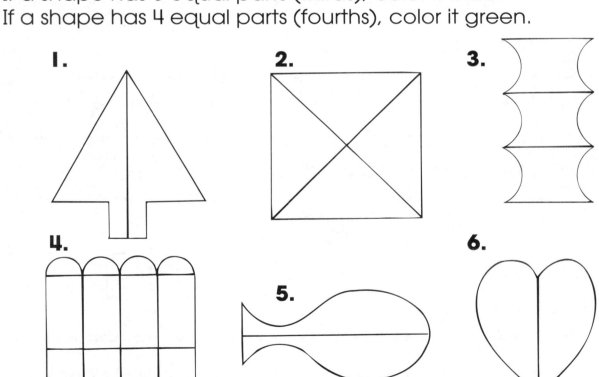

Another way to count by even numbers is to count by twos. Fill in the missing numbers.

1	_____	3	_____	5	_____	7	_____	9	_____
11	_____	13	_____	15	_____	17	_____	19	_____
21	_____	23	_____	25	_____	27	_____	29	_____
31	_____	33	_____	35	_____	37	_____	39	_____
41	_____	43	_____	45	_____	47	_____	49	_____
51	_____	53	_____	55	_____	57	_____	59	_____
61	_____	63	_____	65	_____	67	_____	69	_____
71	_____	73	_____	75	_____	77	_____	79	_____
81	_____	83	_____	85	_____	87	_____	89	_____
91	_____	93	_____	95	_____	97	_____	99	_____

Do More: Count out loud by twos from 2 to 100 (even numbers). Then, count out loud by twos from 1 to 99 (odd numbers).

Directions: Count by 3s. Color the squares with these numbers pink. Tell what pattern you see.

1	2	3	4	5	6	7	8	9	10
11	12	13	14	15	16	17	18	19	20
21	22	23	24	25	26	27	28	29	30
31	32	33	34	35	36	37	38	39	40
41	42	43	44	45	46	47	48	49	50
51	52	53	54	55	56	57	58	59	60
61	62	63	64	65	66	67	68	69	70

Now count by 3s to connect the dots. Use the number chart to help you.

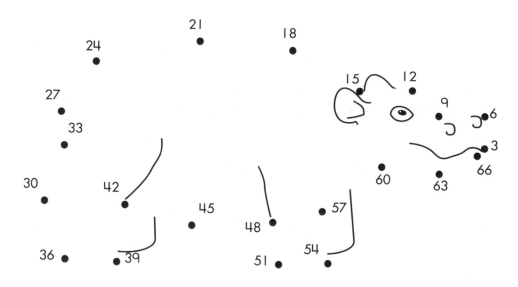

Do More: Count by 4s. Use a red crayon to circle each number in the chart as you count. Tell what pattern you see.

Counting by Fives

Directions: Circle every number that ends with a 5 or a 0. Watch the pattern that develops. The first row has been done for you.

1	2	3	4	⑤	6	7	8	9	⑩
11	12	13	14	15	16	17	18	19	20
21	22	23	24	25	26	27	28	29	30
31	32	33	34	35	36	37	38	39	40
41	42	43	44	45	46	47	48	49	50
51	52	53	54	55	56	57	58	59	60
61	62	63	64	65	66	67	68	69	70
71	72	73	74	75	76	77	78	79	80
81	82	83	84	85	86	87	88	89	90
91	92	93	94	95	96	97	98	99	100

What is the pattern?

Counting With Cookies!

Trace the numbers.

tens   **ones**

2 tens   I one $2\ 1 = 21$

Combine the tens and the ones. The first one has been done for you.

tens	ones

I. 2 tens 8 ones $2\ 8 = 28$ **2.** 8 tens 3 ones $8\ 3 = 83$

3. 4 tens 6 ones $4\ 6 = 46$ **4.** 7 tens 4 ones $7\ 4 = 74$

5. 5 tens 7 ones $5\ 7 = 77$ **6.** I ten 7 ones $1\ 7 = 17$

7. 3 tens 8 ones $8\ 8 = 38$ **8.** 6 tens 3 ones $6\ 3 = 63$

Separate the tens and the ones. The first one has been done for you.

9. 38 = __3__ tens __8__ ones   **10.** 46 = ___ tens ___ ones

II. 57 = ___ tens ___ ones   **12.** 29 = ___ tens ___ ones

13. 15 = ___ tens ___ ones   **14.** 71 = ___ tens ___ ones

15. 65 = ___ tens ___ ones   **16.** 21 = ___ tens ___ ones

Addition Problem Solving

Solve each problem.

1. In Ms. Stevens' class, there are 13 boys and 11 girls. How many students does Ms. Stevens have in all?

_____

2. On Monday, Ms. Brown received 6 apples. On Thursday, 3 more students brought in apples for her. How many apples in all were given to Ms. Brown?

_____

3. One day, 74 kids ordered pizza for lunch and 92 kids ordered a salad. How many kids ordered lunch?

_____

4. Timmy the Trout ate 12 worms on Saturday, 9 worms on Sunday, and 18 worms on Monday. How many worms did he eat all together?

_____

5. Charlie the Chimp found 5 figs on Monday, 2 figs on Wednesday, and 8 figs on Friday. How many figs did he find in all?

_____

6. Bobby read 18 pages of a book on Monday. On Tuesday he read 10 more pages. How many pages did he read in all?

_____

btraction Problem Solving

Read the story. Then, solve each problem.

Lucie and Ken are going grocery shopping. They have to solve math problems as they go. Help Lucie and Ken make their way through the grocery store.

1. Lucie and Ken have 2 tomatoes at home, but they need a total of 7 to make soup. How many tomatoes do they need to buy? They need to buy _____ tomatoes.

2. Lucie and Ken have $15 to spend on groceries. They have already spent $6. How many dollars do Lucie and Ken have left? Lucie and Ken have $_____ left.

3. Lucie picked up 4 onions and Ken picked up 2 onions. How many more onions did Lucie have than Ken? Lucie had _____ more onions than Ken.

4. Lucie and Ken are ready to check out. Line 1 has 8 people waiting to check out. Line 2 has 2 people waiting. How many more people are waiting in Line 1 than in Line 2? There are _____ more people in Line 1.

5. There are 9 pints of chocolate ice cream and 14 pints of vanilla ice cream. How many more pints of vanilla are there? There are _____ more pints of vanilla ice cream.

6. Lucie and Ken have to take a taxi home. There are 12 taxis across the street, but 5 of them are on a break. How many taxis are available? There are _____ taxis available.

More Than

Materials: 100 chart

More than means bigger, so **count forward**.

Find 7 more than 18. AM

11	12	13	14	15	16	17	18	19	20
21	22	23	24	25	26	27	28	29	30

The answer is 25.

1. Find 5 more than 33.

   a. Start on number 33. Count forward or count back?

   _____

   b. Count how many? ☐ The answer is ☐ .

2. Find 6 more than 63.

   a. Start on number ☐ . Count forward or count back?

   _____

   b. Count how many? ☐ The answer is ☐ .

Do More: What type of math problem is counting forward?

66

Less Than

Materials: 100 chart

Less than means smaller, so **count back**.

Find 6 more than 14.

1	2	3	4	5	6	7	8	9	10
11	12	13	14	15	16	17	18	19	20

The answer is 8.

1. Find 9 less than 50.

   a. Start on number 50. Count forward or count back?

   _____

   b. Count how many? ☐ The answer is ☐.

2. Find 12 less than 72.

   a. Start on number ☐. Count forward or count back?

   _____

   b. Count how many? ☐ The answer is ☐.

Do More: What type of math problem is counting back?

Number Construction

Materials: base-ten blocks

1. Find all the 2-digit numbers with digits of 2, 3, and 4.

     __2__   __2__   __2__   __3__   _____   _____

     __3__   __2__   _____   _____   _____   _____

     _____   _____   _____   _____   _____   _____

Circle the ones digits. Put a box around the tens digits.

2. What was the largest number you made?
Build the number with base-ten blocks.

_____

3. What was the smallest number you made?
Build the number with base-ten blocks.

_____

4. How did you find the numbers?

_____

Do More: Find all the 2-digit numbers with digits of 5, 6, and 7.
Tell how you found the numbers.

Great Groups

Materials: counting blocks

1. There are 4 people in the family. Each wants 2 pieces of pie. How many pieces will need to be cut?

    a. Use counting blocks. Make 4 groups of 2. Count the blocks.

    b. ☐ pieces should be cut.

    c. Write a number sentence.

$$\boxed{} + \boxed{} + \boxed{} + \boxed{} = \boxed{}$$

2. On Manuel's street, 5 people have cats. Each person has 2 cats. How many cats live on Manuel's street?

    a. Use counting blocks.

    Make ☐ groups of ☐.

    Count the blocks.

    b. There are ☐ cats.

    c. Write a number sentence. _____

Do More: Tell a story that matches the following number sentence. $6 + 6 + 6 = 18$

Simon Says

Directions: Read each direction and do what Simon says.

1	2							9	
					16				
		23							
				35					
	42								

1. Simon says to fill in the missing numbers in the chart.

2. Simon says circle the number that is one square after 18.

3. Simon says circle the number that is one square before 32.

4. Simon says circle the number that is two squares after 27.

5. Simon says circle the number that is two squares before 15.

6. Simon says circle the number that is four squares after 44.

7. Simon says circle the number that is three squares before 39.

8. Simon says circle the number that is five squares after 18.

Do More: Make up some Simon says directions for the number chart. Have a friend find the correct numbers.

al Patterns

Directions: Use a red crayon and a yellow crayon. Color the six flowers in six different ways. Color each petal one color. All the petals must be colored.

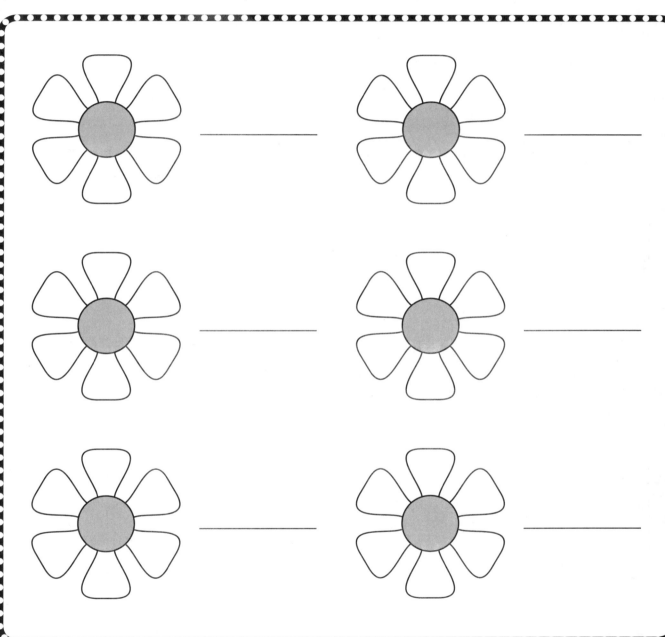

Do More: Number the flowers in order so the red petals show a growing pattern.

A Real Fashion Statement

Directions: Look at each pattern. Use three different colors that you like. Color the scarf in the same pattern.

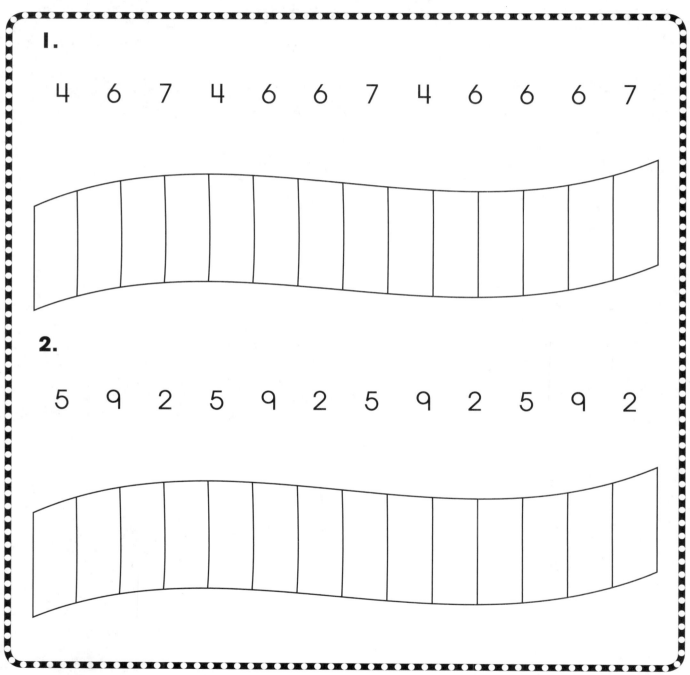

1.

4 6 7 4 6 6 7 4 6 6 6 7

2.

5 9 2 5 9 2 5 9 2 5 9 2

Do More: Look at each pattern. Tell whether it is a repeating pattern or a growing pattern. Explain how you know.

Secret Code

Directions: Some secret codes use the numbers of the letters of the alphabet. Number the letters in order.

A	B	C	D	E	F
1	2				

G	H	I	J	K	L

M	N	O	P	Q	R

S	T	U	V	W	X

Y	Z

Secret Code

Directions: Find the letter for each number on page 73 to unlock the riddle and the answer.

___ ___ ___ ___
23   8   1   20

___ ___ ___ ___ ___ ___ ___
 3   12   15   20   8   5   19

___ ___ ___ ___   ___
 4   15   5   19   1

___ ___ ___ ___ ___
 8   15   21   19   5

___ ___ ___ ___ ?
23   5   1   18

___ ___ ___ ___ ___ ___ ___
 1   4   4   18   5   19   19

Do More: Write three words using the code key. Have a friend unlock your code.

Sum Search

Directions: Work with a partner. Use two different colors of counters. Use the counters to model each addition expression. Match each addition expression with the correct sum. You may use a sum more than once.

1. 8 + 3 =

2. 4 + 6 =

3. 6 + 5 =

4. 3 + 3 =

5. 5 + 4 =

6. 8 + 1 =

7. 6 + 6 =

8. 4 + 3 =

9. 2 + 6 =

10. 3 + 2 =

10
5
9
8
12
6
3
1
11
2
4
7

Do More: Make up addition expressions to match the sums you did not use. How do you know your expression matches the sum?

Difference Search

Directions: Work with a partner. Use two different colors of counters. Use the counters to model each subtraction expression. Match each subtraction expression with the correct difference. You may use a difference more than once.

1. $11 - 3 =$

2. $9 - 9 =$

3. $5 - 3 =$

4. $7 - 4 =$

5. $12 - 2 =$

6. $11 - 6 =$

7. $12 - 1 =$

8. $10 - 7 =$

9. $8 - 3 =$

10. $6 - 0 =$

10
5
9
8
0
6
3
1
11
2
4
7

Do More: Make up subtraction expressions to match the differences you did not use. How do you know your expression matches the difference?

Directions: Use counters to find the sum or difference of each square. Read each clue. Follow the directions. Cross out the squares that will not work. Color the secret square.

1. The secret square does not have a difference of 2.

2. The secret square does not have a sum of 9.

3. The secret square does not have a 7 in the expression.

4. The secret square does not have a difference of 1.

5. The secret square does not have a sum or difference of 4.

6. The secret square does not have a sum or difference of 8.

7. The secret square has the greatest sum remaining.

7 + 3	12 – 4	5 – 4	9 + 2
8 – 4	6 + 3	4 – 2	2 – 0
0 + 4	8 – 1	2 + 8	10 – 7
6 – 5	3 + 4	3 + 5	11 – 6

Do More: How do you know the square you chose is the secret square?

How Can It Be Measured?

Look around the room. Write or draw things in the chart that can be measured in each way.

how tall/long	how wide/thick	how much time	how much space	how heavy

Do More: Which item in your chart fits in the most categories? Are there any two categories that always seem to go together?

How High Will It Go?

Directions: You will need dry rice, a small measuring cup, and a jar with a piece of masking tape from top to bottom.

1. Fill the small cup with rice. Level the top.

Before you pour, guess how high on the tape it will reach.

2. Pour. Was the rice higher or lower than you guessed?_____

3. Fill and pour the small cup three more times.

Guess by drawing on the tape.

Is the rice higher or lower than your mark? _____

Mark the actual level with a line and a 4.

4. Fill and pour the small cup one more time.

Predict by drawing on the tape.

Is the rice higher or lower than your mark? _____

Mark the actual level with a line and a 5.

Stick the tape from the jar on this paper.

Which Holds More?

Materials: 2-liter soda bottle, gallon jug, paper cups, water, sink

Which holds more, the 2-liter soda bottle, or the 1-gallon milk jug?

1. Estimate: _____

Fill the soda bottle with water. Pour the water into cups and empty them into the sink. Count the number of cups.

2. The soda bottle holds _____ cups.

Fill the milk jug with water. Pour the water into cups and empty them into the sink. Count the number of cups.

3. The milk jug holds _____ cups.

4. Which container holds more water? _____

5. How many more cups does it hold? _____

Do More: Tell how to compare the sizes of 2 containers.

Filling a Box

1. Look at a big box. Write about its size.

_____

_____

2. Use a drinking straw ruler. Measure how big the box is around the opening.

Predict: _____ straws   Actual: _____ straws

3. Use a drinking straw ruler to measure how deep the box is.

Predict: _____ straws   Actual: _____ straws

4. What can you use to fill the box?

Predict: _____ units

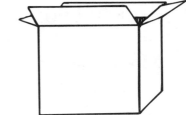

5. Count how many units filled the box.

Actual: _____ units

6. Choose a unit that can cover one side of the box. _____

How many units cover the side? _____

Predict: _____ units   Actual: _____ units

Big Units and Small Units

You will need small blocks and index cards.

1. You will measure the top of your desk. Will it take more index cards or blocks?

   Guess: _____ blocks   _____ cards

   Explain your guess.

2. Cover your desk.

   Actual: _____ blocks   _____ cards

3. You will measure the distance from your desk to the door. Will it take more index cards or blocks?

   Guess: _____ blocks   _____ cards

   Explain your guess.

4. Measure the distance.

   Actual: _____ blocks   _____ cards

Do More: Pretend you put a ball on one side of a balance scale. Will it take more blocks or index cards to balance it?

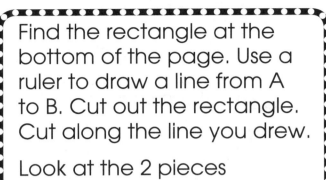

Making Triangles

Find the rectangle at the bottom of the page. Use a ruler to draw a line from A to B. Cut out the rectangle. Cut along the line you drew.

Look at the 2 pieces of the rectangle.

I. What shapes do you have now?

_____

2. How do the pieces compare?

_____

3. Each piece is _____ the size of the rectangle.

Find the square at the bottom of the page. Use a ruler to draw a line from C to D. Cut out the square. Cut along the line you drew.

Look at the 2 pieces of the square.

4. What shapes do you have now?

_____

5. How do the pieces compare?

_____

6. Each piece is _____ the size of the square.

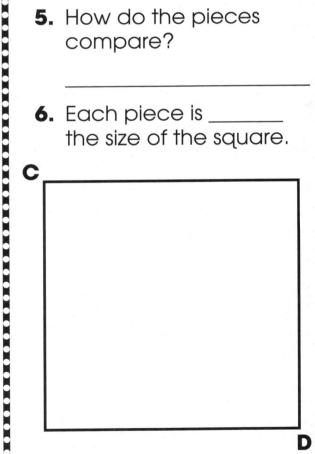

Answer Key

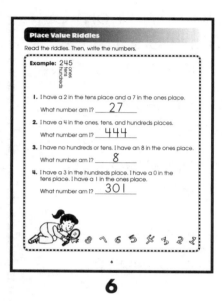

Place Value Riddles

Read the riddles. Then, write the numbers.

Example: 245
ones
tens
hundreds

1. I have a 2 in the tens place and a 7 in the ones place.
   What number am I? __27__

2. I have a 4 in the ones, tens, and hundreds places.
   What number am I? __444__

3. I have no hundreds or tens. I have an 8 in the ones place.
   What number am I? __8__

4. I have a 3 in the hundreds place. I have a 0 in the tens place. I have a 1 in the ones place.
   What number am I? __301__

6

6

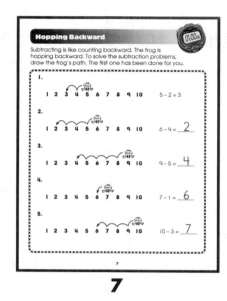

Hopping Backward

Subtracting is like counting backward. The frog is hopping backward. To solve the subtraction problems, draw the frog's path. The first one has been done for you.

1. 1 2 3 4 5 6 7 8 9 10   5 − 2 = 3

2. 1 2 3 4 5 6 7 8 9 10   6 − 4 = __2__

3. 1 2 3 4 5 6 7 8 9 10   9 − 5 = __4__

4. 1 2 3 4 5 6 7 8 9 10   7 − 1 = __6__

5. 1 2 3 4 5 6 7 8 9 10   10 − 3 = __7__

7

7

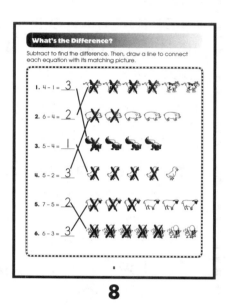

What's the Difference?

Subtract to find the difference. Then, draw a line to connect each equation with its matching picture.

1. 4 − 1 = 3
2. 6 − 4 = 2
3. 5 − 4 = 1
4. 5 − 2 = 3
5. 7 − 5 = 2
6. 6 − 3 = 3

8

8

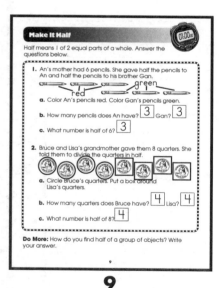

Make It Half

Half means 1 of 2 equal parts of a whole. Answer the questions below.

1. An's mother had 6 pencils. She gave half the pencils to An and half the pencils to his brother Gan.
   red   green
   a. Color An's pencils red. Color Gan's pencils green.
   b. How many pencils does An have? 3 Gan? 3
   c. What number is half of 6? 3

2. Bruce and Lisa's grandmother gave them 8 quarters. She told them to divide the quarters in half.
   a. Circle Bruce's quarters. Put a box around Lisa's quarters.
   b. How many quarters does Bruce have? 4 Lisa? 4
   c. What number is half of 8? 4

Do More: How do you find half of a group of objects? Write your answer.

9

9

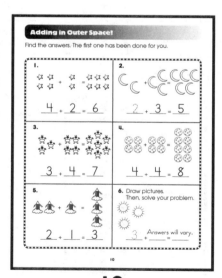

Adding in Outer Space!

Find the answers. The first one has been done for you.

1. __4__ + __2__ = 6

2. __2__ + __3__ = 5

3. __3__ + __4__ = 7

4. __4__ + __4__ = 8

5. __2__ + __1__ = 3

6. Draw pictures. Then, solve your problem.
   __3__ + ____ = ____   Answers will vary.

10

10

Subtraction

Subtract the kites by crossing them out. Write how many are left. Then, color the kites that are left.

9 − 3 = 6

1. 7 − 4 = 3

2. 5 − 4 = 1

3. 8 − 2 = 6

4. 6 − 1 = 5

5. 4 − 2 = 2

6. 8 − 5 = 3

11

11

Answer Key

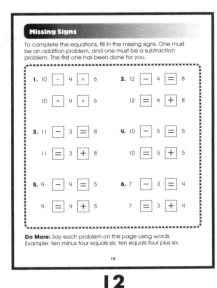

Missing Signs

To complete the equations, fill in the missing signs. One must be an addition problem, and one must be a subtraction problem. The first one has been done for you.

1. $10 - 4 = 6$
   $10 = 4 + 6$

2. $12 - 4 = 8$
   $12 = 4 + 8$

3. $11 - 3 = 8$
   $11 = 3 + 8$

4. $10 - 5 = 5$
   $10 = 5 + 5$

5. $9 - 4 = 5$
   $9 = 4 + 5$

6. $7 - 3 = 4$
   $7 = 3 + 4$

Do More: Say each problem on this page using words. Example: ten minus four equals six; ten equals four plus six.

12

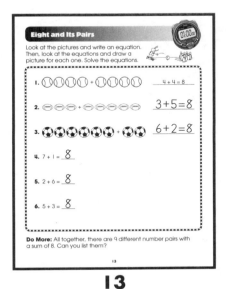

Eight and Its Pairs

Look at the pictures and write an equation. Then, look at the equations and draw a picture for each one. Solve the equations.

1. $4 + 4 = 8$

2. $3 + 5 = 8$

3. $6 + 2 = 8$

4. $7 + 1 = 8$

5. $2 + 6 = 8$

6. $5 + 3 = 8$

Do More: All together, there are 9 different number pairs with a sum of 8. Can you list them?

13

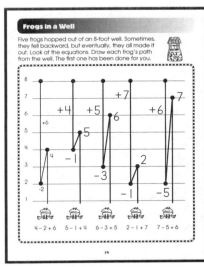

Frogs in a Well

Five frogs hopped out of an 8-foot well. Sometimes, they fell backward, but eventually, they all made it out. Look at the equations. Draw each frog's path from the well. The first one has been done for you.

$4 - 2 + 6$ $5 - 1 + 4$ $6 - 3 + 5$ $2 - 1 + 7$ $7 - 5 + 6$

14

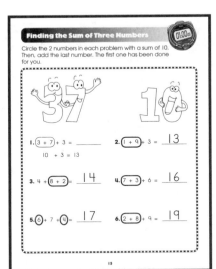

Finding the Sum of Three Numbers

Circle the 2 numbers in each problem with a sum of 10. Then, add the last number. The first one has been done for you.

1. $(3 + 7) + 3 =$ ____
   $10 + 3 = 13$

2. $(1 + 9) + 3 = 13$

3. $4 + (8 + 2) = 14$

4. $(7 + 3) + 6 = 16$

5. $(6) + 7 + (4) = 17$

6. $(2 + 8) + 9 = 19$

15

Which Unit?

Which tool can you use to measure? Circle the best choice.

1. How much does this jar hold?
2. How tall is this doll?
3. How much water?
4. How heavy is this bag of candy?
5. How short is this castle?

16

Inch by Inch

How long is each object? Fill in the missing numbers on the rulers to find out.

1. The pen is __5__ inches long.
   1 2 3 4 **5**

2. The shovel is __6__ inches long.
   2 **4** **6**

3. The chalk is __3__ inches long.
   3 **4** **5** **6**

17

Answer Key

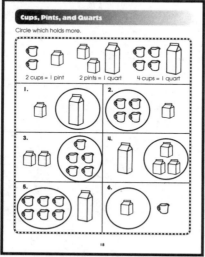

18

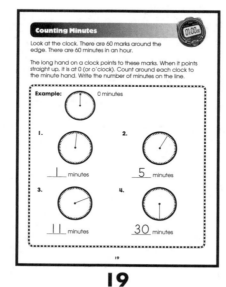

19

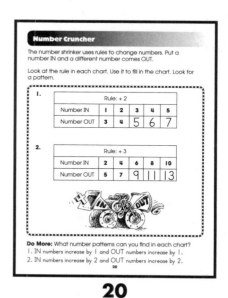

20

Tricky Triangles

These shapes are triangles.

1. How many sides does a triangle have? **3**
2. How many corners does a triangle have? **3**
3. Look for triangles in the picture below. How many triangles can you find? Color each triangle. **10**

21

Find the Circles

Directions: Color all the circles you see in each picture.

Do More: Name an object that you can draw that is shaped like a circle. *Answers will vary.*

22

Find the Squares

Directions: Color all the squares you see in each picture.

Do More: Draw a picture that has a square in it. *Answers will vary.*

23

Answer Key

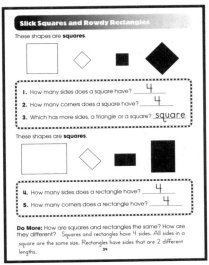

Slick Squares and Rowdy Rectangles

These shapes are **squares**.

1. How many sides does a square have? 4
2. How many corners does a square have? 4
3. Which has more sides, a triangle or a square? square

These shapes are **squares**.

4. How many sides does a rectangle have? 4
5. How many corners does a rectangle have? 4

Do More: How are squares and rectangles the same? How are they different? Squares and rectangles have 4 sides. All sides in a square are the same size. Rectangles have sides that are 2 different lengths.

24

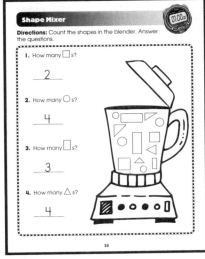

Shape Mixer

Directions: Count the shapes in the blender. Answer the questions.

1. How many ☐ s? 2
2. How many ◯ s? 4
3. How many ▭ s? 3
4. How many △ s? 4

25

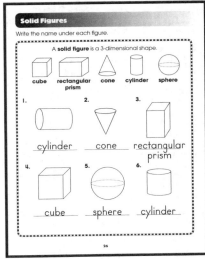

Solid Figures

Write the name under each figure.

A **solid figure** is a 3-dimensional shape.

cube   rectangular prism   cone   cylinder   sphere

1. cylinder
2. cone
3. rectangular prism
4. cube
5. sphere
6. cylinder

26

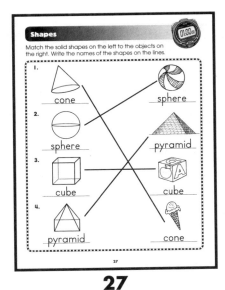

Shapes

Match the solid shapes on the left to the objects on the right. Write the names of the shapes on the lines.

1. cone
2. sphere
3. cube
4. pyramid

sphere
pyramid
cube
cone

27

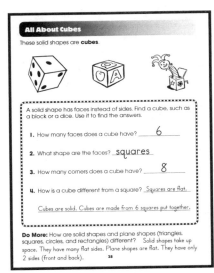

All About Cubes

These solid shapes are **cubes**.

A solid shape has faces instead of sides. Find a cube, such as a block or a dice. Use it to find the answers.

1. How many faces does a cube have? 6
2. What shape are the faces? squares
3. How many corners does a cube have? 8
4. How is a cube different from a square? Squares are flat. Cubes are solid. Cubes are made from 6 squares put together.

Do More: How are solid shapes and plane shapes (triangles, squares, circles, and rectangles) different? Solid shapes take up space. They have many flat sides. Plane shapes are flat. They have only 2 sides (front and back).

28

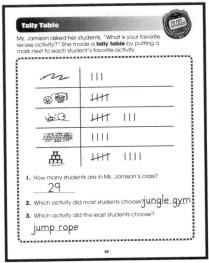

Tally Table

Ms. Jamison asked her students, "What is your favorite recess activity?" She made a **tally table** by putting a mark next to each student's favorite activity.

	III
	₩₩
	₩₩ III
	IIII
	₩₩ IIII

1. How many students are in Ms. Jamison's class? 29
2. Which activity did most students choose? jungle gym
3. Which activity did the least students choose? jump rope

29

Answer Key

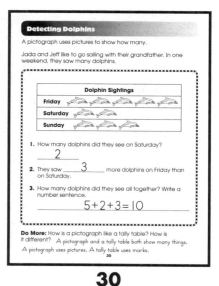

Detecting Dolphins

A pictograph uses pictures to show how many.

Jada and Jeff like to go sailing with their grandfather. In one weekend, they saw many dolphins.

Dolphin Sightings

Friday	🐬 🐬 🐬 🐬 🐬
Saturday	🐬 🐬
Sunday	🐬 🐬 🐬

1. How many dolphins did they see on Saturday?
   __2__

2. They saw __3__ more dolphins on Friday than on Saturday.

3. How many dolphins did they see all together? Write a number sentence.
   __5+2+3=10__

Do More: How is a pictograph like a tally table? How is it different? A pictograph and a tally table both show many things. A pictograph uses pictures. A tally table uses marks.

30

30

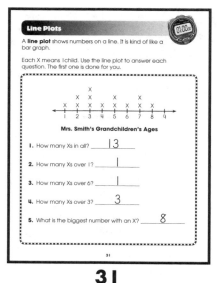

Line Plots

A **line plot** shows numbers on a line. It is kind of like a bar graph.

Each X means 1 child. Use the line plot to answer each question. The first one is done for you.

Mrs. Smith's Grandchildren's Ages

1. How many Xs in all? __13__
2. How many Xs over 1? __1__
3. How many Xs over 6? __1__
4. How many Xs over 3? __3__
5. What is the biggest number with an X? __8__

31

31

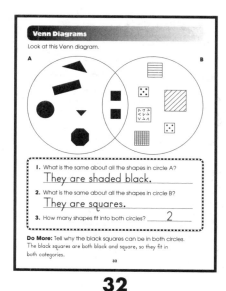

Venn Diagrams

Look at this Venn diagram.

1. What is the same about all the shapes in circle A?
   __They are shaded black.__
2. What is the same about all the shapes in circle B?
   __They are squares.__
3. How many shapes fit into both circles? __2__

Do More: Tell why the black squares can be in both circles. The black squares are both black and square, so they fit in both categories.

32

32

Ladybug Lost

Help the ladybug find her way home. Fill in the missing numbers. Start at the number 1.

	50	49	**48**	47
30	**29**	28	27	**26**	25	46
31	12	11	**10**	**9**	**24**	
32	**13**			8	**23**	**45**
33	14	2		7		44
34	15	**3**	**4**	**5**	22	**43**
35	**16**	17	18	19	**20**	21
36	**37**	38	39	**40**	41	42

34

34

What Number Is Missing?

Write in the missing numbers.

6, 7, _8_

1. 6, _7_, 8	8. _9_, 10	7. _8_, 9
2. 5, _6_, 7	_1_, 2, 3	_4_, 5, 6
3. 1, 2, _3_	_6_, 7, 8	_2_, 3, 4
4. _7_, 8, 9	_5_, 6, 7	2, _3_, 4
5. 4, 5, _6_	2, 3, _4_	7, 8, _9_
6. 3, _4_, 5	_7_, 8, 9	4, _5_, 6
7. 5, 6, _7_	3, 4, _5_	1, _2_, 3
8. 8, 9, _10_	_3_, 4, 5	_8_, 9, 10

35

35

Missing Numbers

1. Ms. Martin had a box of lost hats. On Tuesday, she found 3 more lost hats. She counted 7 hats all together. How many hats did she have on Monday?

   Monday   Tuesday

   a. Draw the missing hats.
   b. Write the number sentence. __4__ + __3__ = __7__

2. Some brown bears are hungry. They join 5 black bears. Now there are 9 bears all together. How many brown bears are there?

   brown bears   black bears

   a. Draw the missing blocks.
   b. Write the number sentence. __4__ + __5__ = __9__

Do More: What words tell you to use an addition problem? The words all together tell you this is an addition problem.

36

36

Answer Key

Missing Numbers

1. The clown at the zoo held 7 balloons. Some of the balloons got loose and floated away. He counted 2 balloons left. How many balloons floated away?

   a. Cross out balloons until only 2 are left. How many did you cross out? 5

   b. Write the number sentence. $7 - 5 = 2$

2. There is a stack of 10 pancakes. Oliver ate some. There were 4 pancakes left. How many did Oliver eat? 6

   a. Cross out counting blocks until only 4 are left. How many did you cross out?

   b. Write the number sentence. $10 - 6 = 4$

Do More: What words tell you to use a subtraction problem? The word **left** tells you this is a subtraction problem.

37

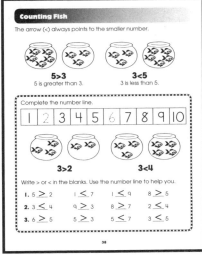

Counting Fish

The arrow (<) always points to the smaller number.

5>3
5 is greater than 3.

3<5
3 is less than 5.

Complete the number line.

| 1 | 2 | 3 | 4 | 5 | 6 | 7 | 8 | 9 | 10 |

3>2

3<4

Write > or < in the blanks. Use the number line to help you.

1. $5 > 2$ $1 < 7$ $1 < 9$ $8 > 5$

2. $3 < 4$ $9 > 3$ $8 > 7$ $2 < 4$

3. $6 > 5$ $5 > 3$ $5 < 7$ $3 < 5$

38

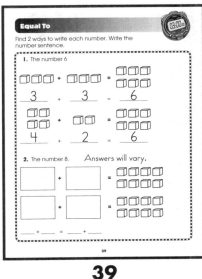

Equal To

Find 2 ways to write each number. Write the number sentence.

1. The number 6

   $3 + 3 = 6$

   $4 + 2 = 6$

2. The number 8.   Answers will vary.

   ___ + ___ = ___ + ___

39

How Many All Together?

1. Chito and Miguel went to a pet store. Chito chose 5 fish. Miguel chose 4 fish. How many fish did they buy **all together**?

   a. Draw the fish. Count all the fish.

   Chito   Miguel

   b. Write the number sentence. $5 + 4 = 9$

2. Angela ate 3 cookies. Cary ate 4 cookies. How many cookies did they eat **all together**?

   | 1 | 2 | 3 | 4 | 5 | 6 | 7 | 8 |

   a. Start on 3 and **count forward** 4 spaces. You will end at number 7

   b. Write the number sentence. $3 + 4 = 7$

Do More: What kind of number sentence do you use to find how many **all together**? Adding number sentences

40

How Many Left?

1. Kessie's rabbit had 6 babies. She finds homes for 3 of the babies. How many baby are **left**?

   a. Cross out the 3 rabbits that have homes. Count the rabbits that are left.

   There are 3 rabbits left.

   b. Write the number sentence. $6 - 3 = 3$

2. Dave has 8 trucks. He gives 3 old trucks to his little brother. How many trucks does he have **left**?

   | 1 | 2 | 3 | 4 | 5 | 6 | 7 | 8 |

   a. Start at 8 on the number line. **Count back** 3 spaces.

   Dave has 5 trucks left.

   b. Write the number sentence. $8 - 3 = 5$

Do More: What kind of number sentence do you use to find how many **left**? Subtracting number sentences

41

How Many Left?

Materials: 100 chart and counting blocks

1. Al has 19 baseball cards. He sold 14 to his friend. How many cards does Al have **left**?

   a. Use the 100 chart. Color the number 19 red.

   Count back or count forward? count back

   Count 14 spaces. Color the number you land on blue.

   Al has 5 baseball cards left.

   b. Write a number sentence. $19 - 14 = 5$

2. Theo has a box of 14 chocolates. Christa eats 5 chocolates. How many chocolates does Theo have **left**?

   a. Use counting blocks. Count out 14 blocks.

   Add 5 blocks or take away 5 blocks? take away

   Count the blocks now. Theo has 9 chocolates left.

   b. Write a number sentence. $14 - 5 = 9$

Do More: Tell a story for this number sentence.

Solve the problem. $9 - 4 = 5$

42

89

Answer Key

How Many Pieces?

Stella has 18 pieces of candy. She wants to share the candy with friends.

1. Stella wants to give 3 pieces of candy to each friend. Circle groups of 3 pieces. Count the number of groups.
   a. How many friends get candy? __6__
   b. Will there be any candy left over? __no__

2. Stella wants to give candy to more people. Should she give fewer pieces to each person, or more pieces to each person? __fewer pieces__

3. What if Stella gives each person 4 pieces? Make each group of 4 pieces a different color.
   a. How many people will get candy? __4__
   b. Will there be any candy left over? __2 pieces left over__

Do More: Should Stella give 3 or 4 pieces to each friend. Why? Answers will vary. Students might choose to have no candy left over, or to have candy left for Stella. Some students might want to give candy to more people. 43

43

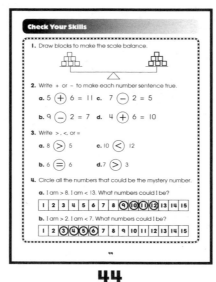

Check Your Skills

1. Draw blocks to make the scale balance.

2. Write + or – to make each number sentence true.
   a. 5 (+) 6 = 11   c. 7 (–) 2 = 5
   b. 9 (–) 2 = 7   d. 4 (+) 6 = 10

3. Write >, <, or =
   a. 8 (>) 5   c. 10 (<) 12
   b. 6 (=) 6   d. 7 (>) 3

4. Circle all the numbers that could be the mystery number.
   a. I am > 8. I am < 13. What numbers could I be?
   1 2 3 4 5 6 7 8 (9)(10)(11)(12) 13 14 15
   b. I am > 2. I am < 7. What numbers could I be?
   1 2 (3)(4)(5)(6) 7 8 9 10 11 12 13 14 15

44

44

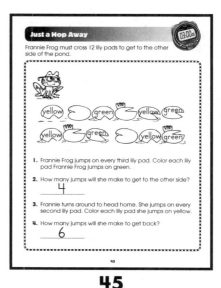

Just a Hop Away

Frannie Frog must cross 12 lily pads to get to the other side of the pond.

yellow green yellow green
yellow green yellow green

1. Frannie Frog jumps on every third lily pad. Color each lily pad Frannie Frog jumps on green.

2. How many jumps will she make to get to the other side?
   __4__

3. Frannie turns around to head home. She jumps on every second lily pad. Color each lily pad she jumps on yellow.

4. How many jumps will she make to get back?
   __6__

45

45

Measuring Fun

Find the answers below. Foxy is running a race.

1. Use small paper clips to measure how far he runs.
   How many paper clips long is the trail?
   __11__

2. Measure the trail using centimeters.
   How many centimeters long is the trail?
   __33__

3. Which way of measuring was easier? Tell why.
   Answers will vary.

A small paper clip is about 3 cm long. Students may count by threes for each paper clip they used to measure the line. ↑

How many centimeters long is a paper clip? How could you use this information to find the trail length in centimeters, without measuring? Write your answers on a separate sheet of paper.

46

46

Making a Prediction

1. Find two containers. Draw the two containers.

2. Use a piece of yarn. Measure how big around on two containers. Predict: Does the one that is bigger around hold more?

   _____

3. Tell how you checked it out.

   _____

Let students come up with their own methods for solving this problem. They will find that there isn't always a connection between distance around and capacity because there are other dimensions that affect capacity.

Do More: Put three containers in order from biggest around to smallest around. Then put them in order from holds most to holds least. Talk about what you noticed.

47

47

"Weighting" in Line

1. Look at the three objects below. Which do you think is heaviest? Which is lightest? Which is in the middle? Number them 1–3 to show lightest to heaviest.
   __3__   __2__   __1__

2. Choose three items in your house. Guess what order they go in.
   Guess:

Allow students to try different methods of comparing the mass of 3 objects. They may compare two on the balance scale then compare the third object to one of those. Make sure that they recheck their order before recording it. Encourage them to explain the steps of the process in detail.

lightest   heaviest

48

48

Answer Key

Plus a Little More (49)

How long is the snake? See that its head does not match up with the tiles.

I. The snake is longer than 5 tiles. It is shorter than 6 tiles.

What can we call that length? $5\frac{1}{2}$ tiles

Let's make a rule: Count the number of units that are **mostly** covered.

Use this rule to name the measurement of each critter.

2. 3 units

4. 4 units

3. 5 units

49

Paper Clip Differences (50)

Directions: Next to each length, write the number of small paper clips that fit on the line. Then write a math sentence in the box that shows the difference between the two lengths.

I.

$4 - 2 = 2$

2.

$3 - 2 = 1$

3.

$5 - 3 = 2$

Do More: Would it be easy to measure things using only paper clips? Why or why not?

50

How Much Space? (51)

I. Look at the shapes. Estimate. Answers will vary.
  a. Which shape has the most space? _____
  b. Which shape has the least space? _____
  c. Do any of the shapes have the same amount of space?

2. Count the squares in each shape to check your estimates.
  Shape A: 14   Shape B: 12
  Shape C: 10   Shape D: 12

3. How close were your estimates? Answers will vary.

Do More: Use grid paper. Draw 2 different shapes that have the same space. Tell how you did this. Answers will vary.

51

Telling Time (52)

Peter is always busy after school and on the weekends with sports and other activities. Look at his schedule below.

7:30 A.M. Homework
10:00 A.M. Piano Lessons
12:30 P.M. Karate Lessons
4:00 P.M. Football Practice
6:30 P.M. Math Tutoring
9:15 P.M. Reading

Label each clock with the time and the activity it is showing.

I. 4:00 football practice
2. 6:30 math tutoring
3. 10:00 piano lessons
4. 7:30 homework
5. 9:15 reading
6. 12:30 karate lessons

52

The Time Is? (53)

I. Kenny's birthday party started at 1:00.
  a. Show this time on the clock. — Start Time
  b. The party ended at 4:00. Show the time on the clock. — End Time
  c. How many hours did the party last? 3

2. Eric's soccer game starts at 10:00.
  a. Show the time on the clock. — Start Time
  b. After the game, Eric watched his brother's game. He left at 1:00. Show the time. — End Time
  c. How many hours was Eric at the soccer field? 3

Do More: How did you find the number of hours? Answers will vary.

53

How Long? (54)

I. The parade started at 9:00 A.M.
  a. Show this time on the clock. — Start Time
  b. It lasted 2 hours. Show the time the parade ended. — End Time
  c. How did you solve this problem? count backward 2 hours

2. Misha went to the park to play. She played for 3 hours with her friends. It was 4:00 when she went home. — End Time
  a. Show this time on the clock.
  b. What time did Misha get to the park? 1:00
  c. How did you solve the problem? count backward 3 hours

54

Answer Key

Reading a Bar Graph

Look at the **bar graph**. Use it to answer the questions.

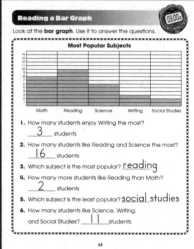

Most Popular Subjects

1. How many students enjoy Writing the most?
   __3__ students

2. How many students like Reading and Science the most?
   __16__ students

3. Which subject is the most popular? __reading__

4. How many more students like Reading than Math?
   __2__ students

5. Which subject is the least popular? __social studies__

6. How many students like Science, Writing, and Social Studies? __11__ students

55

Copycat

Directions: The part of the pattern that repeats is shown. Draw the pattern.

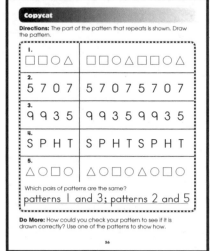

Which pairs of patterns are the same?
patterns 1 and 3; patterns 2 and 5

Do More: How could you check your pattern to see if it is drawn correctly? Use one of the patterns to show how.

56

Twice as Nice

Double means add the same amount again.

1. There are 5 triangles. How many triangles will there be if the amount is doubled?

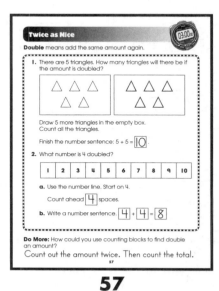

   Draw 5 more triangles in the empty box.
   Count all the triangles.
   Finish the number sentence: 5 + 5 = [10]

2. What number is 4 doubled?

   | 1 | 2 | 3 | 4 | 5 | 6 | 7 | 8 | 9 | 10 |

   a. Use the number line. Start on 4.
      Count ahead [4] spaces.

   b. Write a number sentence. [4] + [4] = [8]

Do More: How could you use counting blocks to find double an amount?
Count out the amount twice. Then count the total.

57

Halves, Thirds, and Fourths

How many equal parts are in each shape?

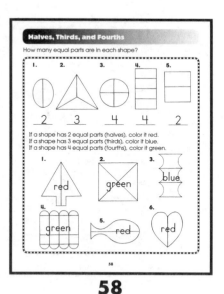

2   3   4   4   2

If a shape has 2 equal parts (halves), color it red.
If a shape has 3 equal parts (thirds), color it blue.
If a shape has 4 equal parts (fourths), color it green.

1. red   2. green   3. blue
4. green   5. red   6. red

58

Counting by Twos

Another way to count by even numbers is to count by twos. Fill in the missing numbers.

1	**2**	3	**4**	5	**6**	7	**8**	9	**10**
11	**12**	13	**14**	15	**16**	17	**18**	19	**20**
21	**22**	23	**24**	25	**26**	27	**28**	29	**30**
31	**32**	33	**34**	35	**36**	37	**38**	39	**40**
41	**42**	43	**44**	45	**46**	47	**48**	49	**50**
51	**52**	53	**54**	55	**56**	57	**58**	59	**60**
61	**62**	63	**64**	65	**66**	67	**68**	69	**70**
71	**72**	73	**74**	75	**76**	77	**78**	79	**80**
81	**82**	83	**84**	85	**86**	87	**88**	89	**90**
91	**92**	93	**94**	95	**96**	97	**98**	99	**100**

Do More: Count out loud by twos from 2 to 100 (even numbers). Then, count out loud by twos from 1 to 99 (odd numbers).

60

One, Two, Three

Directions: Count by 3s. Color the squares with these numbers pink. Tell what pattern you see.

1	2	3	4	5	6	7	8	9	10
11	12	13	14	15	16	17	18	19	20
21	22	23	24	25	26	27	28	29	30
31	32	33	34	35	36	37	38	39	40
41	42	43	44	45	46	47	48	49	50
51	52	53	54	55	56	57	58	59	60
61	62	63	64	65	66	67	68	69	70

Now count by 3s to connect the dots. Use the number chart to help you.

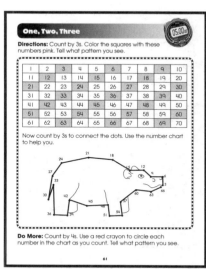

Do More: Count by 4s. Use a red crayon to circle each number in the chart as you count. Tell what pattern you see.

61

Answer Key

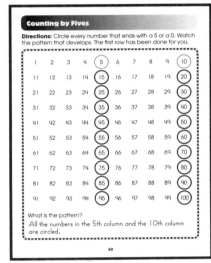

Counting by Fives

Directions: Circle every number that ends with a 5 or a 0. Watch the pattern that develops. The first row has been done for you.

1	2	3	4	(5)	6	7	8	9	(10)
11	12	13	14	(15)	16	17	18	19	(20)
21	22	23	24	(25)	26	27	28	29	(30)
31	32	33	34	(35)	36	37	38	39	(40)
41	42	43	44	(45)	46	47	48	49	(50)
51	52	53	54	(55)	56	57	58	59	(60)
61	62	63	64	(65)	66	67	68	69	(70)
71	72	73	74	(75)	76	77	78	79	(80)
81	82	83	84	(85)	86	87	88	89	(90)
91	92	93	94	(95)	96	97	98	99	(100)

What is the pattern?
All the numbers in the 5th column and the 10th column are circled.

62

62

Counting With Cookies!

Trace the numbers.

tens   ones   2 tens   1 one   21 = 21

Combine the tens and the ones. The first one has been done for you.

tens ones
1. 2 tens 8 ones 28 = 28   2. 8 tens 3 ones 83 = 83
3. 4 tens 6 ones 46 = 46   4. 7 tens 4 ones 74 = 74
5. 5 tens 7 ones 57 = 57   6. 1 ten 7 ones 17 = 17
7. 3 tens 8 ones 38 = 38   8. 6 tens 3 ones 63 = 63

Separate the tens and the ones. The first one has been done for you.

9. 38 = 3 tens 8 ones   10. 46 = 4 tens 6 ones
11. 57 = 5 tens 7 ones   12. 29 = 2 tens 9 ones
13. 15 = 1 tens 5 ones   14. 71 = 7 tens 1 ones
15. 65 = 6 tens 5 ones   16. 21 = 2 tens 1 ones

63

63

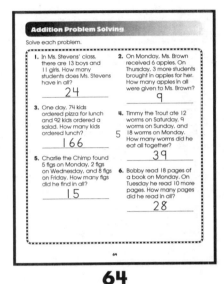

Addition Problem Solving

Solve each problem.

1. In Ms. Stevens' class, there are 13 boys and 11 girls. How many students does Ms. Stevens have in all?
24

2. On Monday, Ms. Brown received 6 apples. On Thursday, 3 more students brought in apples for her. How many apples in all were given to Ms. Brown?
9

3. One day, 74 kids ordered pizza for lunch and 92 kids ordered a salad. How many kids ordered lunch?
166

4. Timmy the Trout ate 12 worms on Saturday, 9 worms on Sunday, and 18 worms on Monday. How many worms did he eat all together?
39

5. Charlie the Chimp found 5 figs on Monday, 2 figs on Wednesday, and 8 figs on Friday. How many figs did he find in all?
15

6. Bobby read 18 pages of a book on Monday. On Tuesday he read 10 more pages. How many pages did he read in all?
28

64

64

Subtraction Problem Solving

Read the story. Then, solve each problem.

Lucie and Ken are going grocery shopping. They have to solve math problems as they go. Help Lucie and Ken make their way through the grocery store.

1. Lucie and Ken have 2 tomatoes at home, but they need a total of 7 to make soup. How many tomatoes do they need to buy? They need to buy 5 tomatoes.

2. Lucie and Ken have $15 to spend on groceries. They have already spent $6. How many dollars do Lucie and Ken have left? Lucie and Ken have $9 left.

3. Lucie picked up 4 onions and Ken picked up 2 onions. How many more onions did Lucie have than Ken? Lucie had 2 more onions than Ken.

4. Lucie and Ken are ready to check out. Line 1 has 8 people waiting to check out. Line 2 has 2 people waiting. How many more people are waiting in Line 1 than in Line 2? There are 6 more people in Line 1.

5. There are 9 pints of chocolate ice cream and 14 pints of vanilla ice cream. How many more pints of vanilla are there? There are 5 more pints of vanilla ice cream.

6. Lucie and Ken have to take a taxi home. There are 12 taxis across the street, but 5 of them are on a break. How many taxis are available? There are 7 taxis available.

65

65

More Than

Materials: 100 chart

More than means bigger, so **count forward**.

Find 7 more than 18. AM

| 11 | 12 | 13 | 14 | 15 | 16 | 17 | 18 | 19 | 20 |
| 21 | 22 | 23 | 24 | (25) | 26 | 27 | 28 | 29 | 30 |

The answer is 25.

1. Find 5 more than 33.
   a. Start on number 33. Count forward or count back?
   forward
   b. Count how many? 5   The answer is 38.

2. Find 6 more than 63.
   a. Start on number 63. Count forward or count back?
   forward
   b. Count how many? 6   The answer is 69.

Do More: What type of math problem is counting forward?
addition

66

66

Less Than

Materials: 100 chart

Less than means smaller, so **count back**.

Find 6 more than 14.

| 1 | 2 | 3 | 4 | 5 | 6 | 7 | (8) | 9 | 10 |
| 11 | 12 | 13 | 14 | 15 | 16 | 17 | 18 | 19 | 20 |

The answer is 8.

1. Find 9 less than 50.
   a. Start on number 50. Count forward or count back?
   back
   b. Count how many? 9   The answer is 41.

2. Find 12 less than 72.
   a. Start on number 72. Count forward or count back?
   back
   b. Count how many? 12   The answer is 60.

Do More: What type of math problem is counting back?
subtraction

67

67

Answer Key

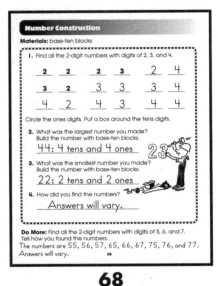

Number Construction

Materials: base-ten blocks

1. Find all the 2-digit numbers with digits of 2, 3, and 4.

2 **2**   **2** **3**   2 4

3 **2**   3 3   3 4

4 2   4 3   4 4

Circle the ones digits. Put a box around the tens digits.

2. What was the largest number you made? Build the number with base-ten blocks.

44: 4 tens and 4 ones

3. What was the smallest number you made? Build the number with base-ten blocks.

22: 2 tens and 2 ones

4. How did you find the numbers?

Answers will vary.

Do More: Find all the 2-digit numbers with digits of 5, 6, and 7. Tell how you found the numbers.
The numbers are 55, 56, 57, 65, 66, 67, 75, 76, and 77. Answers will vary.

68

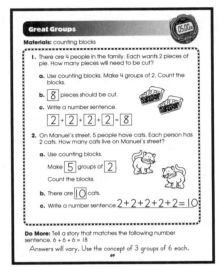

Great Groups

Materials: counting blocks

1. There are 4 people in the family. Each wants 2 pieces of pie. How many pieces will need to be cut?

   a. Use counting blocks. Make 4 groups of 2. Count the blocks.

   b. 8 pieces should be cut.

   c. Write a number sentence.

   2 + 2 + 2 + 2 = 8

2. On Manuel's street, 5 people have cats. Each person has 2 cats. How many cats live on Manuel's street?

   a. Use counting blocks.

   Make 5 groups of 2

   Count the blocks.

   b. There are 10 cats.

   c. Write a number sentence. 2 + 2 + 2 + 2 + 2 = 10

Do More: Tell a story that matches the following number sentence. 6 + 6 + 6 = 18
Answers will vary. Use the concept of 3 groups of 6 each.

69

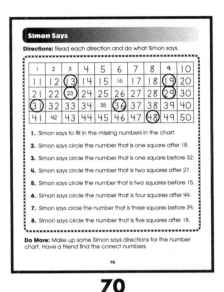

Simon Says

Directions: Read each direction and do what Simon says.

1	2	3	4	5	6	7	8	9	10
11	12	13	14	15	16	17	18	19	20
21	22	23	24	25	26	27	28	29	30
31	32	33	34	35	36	37	38	39	40
41	42	43	44	45	46	47	48	49	50

1. Simon says to fill in the missing numbers in the chart.
2. Simon says circle the number that is one square after 18.
3. Simon says circle the number that is one square before 32.
4. Simon says circle the number that is two squares after 27.
5. Simon says circle the number that is two squares before 15.
6. Simon says circle the number that is four squares after 44.
7. Simon says circle the number that is three squares before 39.
8. Simon says circle the number that is five squares after 18.

Do More: Make up some Simon says directions for the number chart. Have a friend find the correct numbers.

70

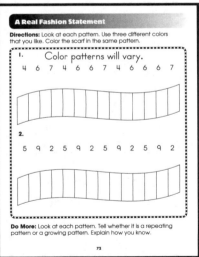

Petal Patterns

Directions: Use a red crayon and a yellow crayon. Color the six flowers in six different ways. Color each petal one color. All the petals must be colored.

1   2   3   4   5   6

Do More: Number the flowers in order so the red petals show a growing pattern.

71

A Real Fashion Statement

Directions: Look at each pattern. Use three different colors that you like. Color the scarf in the same pattern.

1. Color patterns will vary.
4 6 7 4 6 6 7 4 6 6 7

2.
5 9 2 5 9 2 5 9 2 5 9 2

Do More: Look at each pattern. Tell whether it is a repeating pattern or a growing pattern. Explain how you know.

72

Secret Code

Directions: Some secret codes use the numbers of the letters of the alphabet. Number the letters in order.

A	B	C	D	E	F
1	2	3	4	5	6

G	H	I	J	K	L
7	8	9	10	11	12

M	N	O	P	Q	R
13	14	15	16	17	18

S	T	U	V	W	X
19	20	21	22	23	24

Y	Z
25	26

Secret Code

73

Answer Key

Secret Code (cont.)

Directions: Find the letter for each number on page 73 to unlock the riddle and the answer.

```
W   H   A   T
23  8   1   20

C   L   O   T   H   E   S
3   12  15  20  8   5   19

D   O   E   S        A
4   15  5   19       1

H   O   U   S   E
8   15  21  19  5

W   E   A   R  ,
23  5   1   18

A   D   D   R   E   S   S
1   4   4   18  5   19  19
```

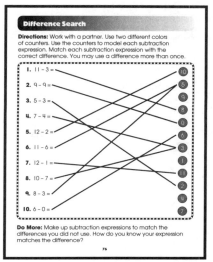

Do More: Write three words using the code key. Have a friend unlock your code.

74

74

Sum Search

Directions: Work with a partner. Use two different colors of counters. Use the counters to model each addition expression. Match each addition expression with the correct sum. You may use a sum more than once.

1. 8 + 3 =
2. 4 + 6 =
3. 6 + 5 =
4. 3 + 3 =
5. 5 + 4 =
6. 8 + 1 =
7. 6 + 6 =
8. 4 + 3 =
9. 2 + 6 =
10. 3 + 2 =

(10, 5, 9, 8, 12, 6, 1, 11, 2, 4, 7)

Do More: Make up addition expressions to match the sums you did not use. How do you know your expression matches the sum?

75

75

Difference Search

Directions: Work with a partner. Use two different colors of counters. Use the counters to model each subtraction expression. Match each subtraction expression with the correct difference. You may use a difference more than once.

1. 11 − 3 =
2. 9 − 9 =
3. 5 − 3 =
4. 7 − 4 =
5. 12 − 2 =
6. 11 − 6 =
7. 12 − 1 =
8. 10 − 7 =
9. 8 − 3 =
10. 6 − 0 =

(10, 5, 9, 8, 0, 6, 3, 1, 2, 4, 7)

Do More: Make up subtraction expressions to match the differences you did not use. How do you know your expression matches the difference?

76

76

Follow the Clues

Directions: Use counters to find the sum or difference of each square. Read each clue. Follow the directions. Cross out the squares that will not work. Color the secret square.

1. The secret square does not have a difference of 2.
2. The secret square does not have a sum of 9.
3. The secret square does not have a 7 in the expression.
4. The secret square does not have a difference of 1.
5. The secret square does not have a sum or difference of 4.
6. The secret square does not have a sum or difference of 8.
7. The secret square has the greatest sum remaining.

7 X 3	12 X 4	5 X 4	9 + 2
8 X 4	6 X 3	4 X 2	2 X 0
0 X 4	8 X 1	2 X 8	10 X 7
6 X 5	3 X 4	3 X 5	11 X 6

Do More: How do you know the square you chose is the secret square?

77

77

How Can It Be Measured?

Look around the room. Write or draw things in the chart that can be measured in each way.

how tall/long	how wide/thick	how much time	how much space	how heavy
Students will recognize that objects have different measurable attributes. Some attributes seem to go hand in hand, such as length and width. Time seems to stand alone. Encourage students to look for more objects even as their charts fill up.				

Do More: Which item in your chart fits in the most categories? Are there any two categories that always seem to go together?

78

78

How High Will It Go?

Directions: You will need dry rice, a small measuring cup, and a jar with a piece of masking tape from top to bottom.

Answers will vary. Students gain experience with the process of comparing volume. If the jar is straight-sided, the marks will be evenly spaced.

Guess by drawing on the tape.

Is the rice higher or lower than your mark? _____

Mark the actual level with a line and a 4.

4. Fill and pour the small cup one more time.

Predict by drawing on the tape.

Is the rice higher or lower than your mark? _____

Mark the actual level with a line and a 5.

Stick the tape from the jar on this paper.

79

79

95

Answer Key

Which Holds More?

Materials: 2-liter soda bottle, gallon jug, paper cups, water, sink

Which holds more, the 2-liter soda bottle, or the 1-gallon milk jug?

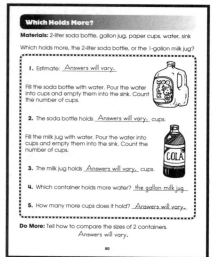

1. Estimate: <u>Answers will vary.</u>

Fill the soda bottle with water. Pour the water into cups and empty them into the sink. Count the number of cups.

2. The soda bottle holds <u>Answers will vary.</u> cups.

Fill the milk jug with water. Pour the water into cups and empty them into the sink. Count the number of cups.

3. The milk jug holds <u>Answers will vary.</u> cups.

4. Which container holds more water? <u>the gallon milk jug</u>

5. How many more cups does it hold? <u>Answers will vary.</u>

Do More: Tell how to compare the sizes of 2 containers. Answers will vary.

80

Filling a Box

1. Look at a big box. Write about its size.
   Students describe all the measureable attributes of the box. Challenge them to propose a method of weighing the box as well.

2. Use a drinking straw ruler. Measure how big the box is around the opening.

   Predict: _____ straws   Actual: _____ straws

3. Use a drinking straw ruler to measure how deep the box is.

   Predict: _____ straws   Actual: _____ straws

4. What can you use to fill the box?

   Predict: _____ units

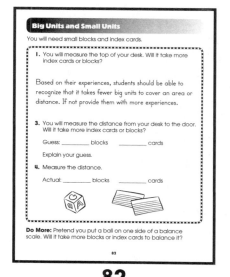

5. Count how many units filled the box.

   Actual: _____ units

6. Choose a unit that can cover one side of the box. _____

   How many units cover the side? _____

   Predict: _____ units   Actual: _____ units

81

Big Units and Small Units

You will need small blocks and index cards.

1. You will measure the top of your desk. Will it take more index cards or blocks?

   Based on their experiences, students should be able to recognize that it takes fewer big units to cover an area or distance. If not provide them with more experiences.

3. You will measure the distance from your desk to the door. Will it take more index cards or blocks?

   Guess: _____ blocks _____ cards

   Explain your guess.

4. Measure the distance.

   Actual: _____ blocks _____ cards

Do More: Pretend you put a ball on one side of a balance scale. Will it take more blocks or index cards to balance it?

82

Making Triangles

Find the rectangle at the bottom of the page. Use a ruler to draw a line from A to B. Cut out the rectangle. Cut along the line you drew.

Look at the 2 pieces of the rectangle.

1. What shapes do you have now?
   <u>2 triangles</u>

2. How do the pieces compare?
   <u>same size and shape</u>

3. Each piece is <u>half</u> the size of the rectangle.

Find the square at the bottom of the page. Use a ruler to draw a line from C to D. Cut out the square. Cut along the line you drew.

Look at the 2 pieces of the square.

4. What shapes do you have now?
   <u>2 triangles</u>

5. How do the pieces compare?
   <u>same size and shape</u>

6. Each piece is <u>half</u> the size of the square.

83